Presented to

....

By

....

Date

....

T0016536

Girl,
Persist in Prayer

CAREY SCOTT

Girl,
Persist in
Prayer

DEVOTIONS
for a
COURAGEOUS FAITH

BARBOUR
PUBLISHING

Published by Barbour Publishing, Inc., 1810 Barbour Drive, Uhrichsville, Ohio 44683, www.barbourbooks.com

Our mission is to inspire the world with the life-changing message of the Bible.

ecpa Member of the
Evangelical Christian
Publishers Association

Printed in China.

Introduction

First Thessalonians 5:17 (TPT) says to "make your life a prayer." This verse is encouraging a continual conversation with God through your words and actions every day. And as followers of Christ, we should accept this privilege with passion and purpose.

The truth is that prayer is a gift to the believer! Not only is it a direct connection to your heavenly Father, but it's also a powerful tool to build your faith. The more you spend time talking to God, the more you'll begin to trust that He is *with* you and *for* you. And persistent prayer is how you create an unshakable foundation of belief because you know God is always listening. Even more, this truth will embolden you as it grows your confidence in His goodness.

If you want to live your one and only life with courageous faith, let prayer be your daily commitment. Talk to God honestly and often. And watch how prayer deepens your love and dependence on the One who created you and delights in who He made you to be.

BELIEVING PRAYER

*Jesus was matter-of-fact: "Yes—and if you embrace
this kingdom life and don't doubt God, you'll not
only do minor feats like I did to the fig tree, but also
triumph over huge obstacles. This mountain, for
instance, you'll tell, 'Go jump in the lake,' and it will
jump. Absolutely everything, ranging from small
to large, as you make it a part of your believing
prayer, gets included as you lay hold of God."*
MATTHEW 21:21–22 MSG

We're told to pray in earnest and believe. Scripture
says that when we choose to trust God with all our
hearts, we'll find victory over big and small things.
When we don't give in to doubt but settle in our
minds that through faith everything is possible,
power is unlocked in our lives.

Does your marriage need renewal? Your health
restoration? Your thought life retraining? Pray,
believing these things will come to pass, and trust
God. Be confident that the answers will come at
the right time and in the right way, glorifying God
and benefiting you.

*Dear God, cultivate in me believing prayers.
Help me trust that Your responses will
be perfect, timely, and always based in
unfailing love. In Jesus' name I pray. Amen.*

IMPOSSIBLE WITHOUT FAITH

Without faith living within us it would be impossible to please God. For we come to God in faith knowing that he is real and that he rewards the faith of those who passionately seek him.

HEBREWS 11:6 TPT

When you activate your faith, pursuing a deeper relationship with God, you please Him. God wants you to know Him more each day. He wants your heart to be open to His will for your life. His hope is that you pursue the design He planned for you to follow. And every choice you make that glorifies His name brings great delight!

Start your day by asking God to increase your faith since you know having faith is vital to pleasing your Father. And then let Him be a part of every decision, every strategy, every frustration, and every celebration throughout your day. Live with a passionate faith for the One who created you!

Dear God, my heart's desire is to please You with my life and glorify Your name. Take every opportunity to grow my faith so it's firmly planted in You, unshakable no matter what comes my way. In Jesus' name I pray. Amen.

YOUR FAITH IS INSTRUMENTAL

But how can people call for help if they don't know who to trust? And how can they know who to trust if they haven't heard of the One who can be trusted? And how can they hear if nobody tells them? And how is anyone going to tell them, unless someone is sent to do it?
ROMANS 10:14–15 MSG

Have you ever considered that maybe your faith can be instrumental in someone else becoming a believer? How will certain people know God is trustworthy unless they see it play out in your life? How will they even know to call on His name in times of trouble?

Ask God for courage to be authentic with others about your belief in Him. Ask for confidence to open up and let those around you take a peek inside your journey of faith. It's okay that your faith isn't perfect, but let them recognize that it is purposeful. We're most often encouraged by seeing rather than hearing. Be willing to let people in.

Dear God, I struggle with trusting others, but I know I can trust You. Build my courage to live authentically. In Jesus' name I pray. Amen.

THE RELATIONSHIP BETWEEN HOPE AND FAITH

Now faith brings our hopes into reality and becomes the foundation needed to acquire the things we long for. It is all the evidence required to prove what is still unseen. This testimony of faith is what previous generations were commended for.
HEBREWS 11:1–2 TPT

Let our hope be anchored in God alone because nothing else is trustworthy. Even with the best intentions, our families will let us down. Even when trying their very best, our friends can't magically make things happen for us. But when we decide that God is our source—that He is the One to make our hopes a reality—we can exhale. We can be at peace.

The world offers many things that promise happiness, wealth, companionship, and healing. Quick fixes are always available. And honestly, we've all fallen prey to clever marketing schemes. But faith in God alone brings hope to life.

Dear God, I realize You are my source for everything I need. From hope to healing to happiness, it's all in Your capable and loving hands. In Jesus' name I pray. Amen.

WHAT ARE YOUR MOUNTAINS?

*Jesus replied, "Let the faith of God be in you!
Listen to the truth I speak to you: Whoever
says to this mountain with great faith and does
not doubt, 'Mountain, be lifted up and thrown
into the midst of the sea,' and believes that
what he says will happen, it will be done."*
MARK 11:22–23 TPT

We all have a mountain in our way. It may be a huge financial peak. It may be betrayal or rejection from someone you deeply trusted. It might be a sense of self-loathing you can't seem to get past. Maybe it's a situation that feels overwhelming to navigate or a relationship you can't repair. Or perhaps it's a diagnosis that has shattered every ounce of hope you were clinging to.

Let today's scripture be what challenges you to pray bold, believing prayers. Activate your faith in God's sovereignty so your doubts lose their power. And let nothing distract you from harnessing the power promised to you through the Lord and commanding those mountains to move!

Dear God, I believe that with You I can move every mountain in my way! In Jesus' name I pray. Amen.

BECOMING A BOLD BELIEVER

*"This is the reason I urge you to boldly believe
for whatever you ask for in prayer—be convinced
that you have received it and it will be yours."*
MARK 11:24 TPT

The kind of faith that Jesus talked about feels too vulnerable at times because we're afraid of being let down. We worry that unanswered requests may cause us to lose faith. Maybe we don't want to be let down again or feel unheard. And what if we pray boldly and fully believe yet don't see what we desperately wanted to see come to pass?

Faith means we trust God no matter what. It means we believe that His way is the best way even if it's not our way. It means we surrender to His timing even when it's drastically different than ours. And so maybe our prayer should be that we learn to exercise our faith in little things so that it becomes stronger. Our faith will increase as we exercise it, just as our muscles become stronger when we exercise them.

*Dear God, help me know deep in my heart that
You not only hear every prayer but also answer in
Your perfect ways—ways that always glorify You
and benefit me. In Jesus' name I pray. Amen.*

PURSUING THE TRUTH

Through faith we understand that the universe was created by the word of God; everything we now see was fashioned from that which is invisible.
HEBREWS 11:3 VOICE

There are lots of crazy ideas about how the earth was created, right? And while today's verse may not be a hard sell for believers, the reality is that countless lies are circulating in the world about God and His works. Unless you spend time in the Word, you will struggle to know the truth when lies come your way.

If you want to grow deeper in your faith and have more confidence and courage to walk it out every day, commit to knowing God's Word. Pursue the truth daily so you don't fall prey to the enemy's plan for chaos and confusion. And make your faith a priority so nothing else eclipses its importance in how you live your life.

Dear God, plant in me a deep love for Your Word! Give me an unshakable desire to pursue truth above all else. And let my life always be an encouragement for others to do the same. In Jesus' name I pray. Amen.

GRACE VERSUS WORK

For by grace you have been saved by faith. Nothing
you did could ever earn this salvation, for it was
the love gift from God that brought us to Christ!
So no one will ever be able to boast, for salvation is
never a reward for good works or human striving.

EPHESIANS 2:8–9 TPT

What a blessed relief to know we are unable to earn
our salvation. We live in a world that is undeniably
achievement driven, making us conditioned from
childhood to work for what we want. Whether we
like it or not, we often thrive on competition, trying
to beat out the next person. And many of us work
ourselves to the bone.

Meditate on grace versus work and talk to
God about what each means to you. Spend time
thanking Him for understanding the limitations of
your humanity and the inability for you to ever be
good enough on your own.

Dear God, forgive me for not understanding the
depth and beauty of grace. I'm humbled by Your
gift of salvation through faith, and I'm forever
grateful You never expected me to earn my
way to eternity. In Jesus' name I pray. Amen.

GOING WHERE CALLED

By faith Abraham heard God's call to travel to a place he would one day receive as an inheritance; and he obeyed, not knowing where God's call would take him. By faith he journeyed to the land of the promise as a foreigner; he lived in tents, as did Isaac and Jacob, his fellow heirs to the promise.
HEBREWS 11:8–9 VOICE

Imagine the amount of faith Abraham had to do what God asked! He was comfortable and wealthy and established, but God had other plans. When He commanded Abraham to pack up and leave his home, Abraham didn't hesitate. He obeyed without knowing where he would end up. Abraham didn't know what kind of life he'd have. But none of that mattered because God spoke.

You can have an unshakable foundation of faith like Abraham. You can live unafraid of following His will. How? Faith. Because Abraham knew God's plans were for good and could be trusted, he didn't hesitate. Ask God to give you steadfast faith to go where He calls you to go.

Dear God, embolden my belief to follow You anywhere at any time. In Jesus' name I pray. Amen.

THE MYTHS OF FORGIVENESS

*"Whenever you stand praying, if you find that
you carry something in your heart against
another person, release him and forgive
him so that your Father in heaven will also
release you and forgive you of your faults."*
MARK 11:25 TPT

When you're struggling with unforgiveness, have an honest conversation with God. The only reason we'd not extend grace is because we don't understand what it means. So often we think forgiving means letting the other person off the hook. Or we think it negates the pain we felt. But neither of those ideas is true.

When you choose to forgive someone, you are securing your own freedom. But living offended keeps you from liberty. God wants you to release others so that He can release you of your sins through faith in Jesus.

*Dear God, give me insight to understand
the dangers of unforgiveness so I'm quick
to extend grace to those who have hurt
me. I don't want to live in the bondage
of offense. In Jesus' name I pray. Amen.*

JUST PASSING THROUGH

*That's why we're always full of courage. Even
while we're at home in the body, we're homesick
to be with the Master—for we live by faith,
not by what we see with our eyes. We live
with a joyful confidence, yet at the same time
we take delight in the thought of leaving our
bodies behind to be at home with the Lord.*

2 CORINTHIANS 5:6–8 TPT

As believers, we should have a longing for heaven
while we're walking out our faith here. There are
some beautiful things in this world, but once we
take our final breath on earth, none of those things
goes with us to heaven. And while we have divinely
inspired work to do, this is neither our home nor
our final destination.

That's why we can live with courage and confidence! We know better things are coming. We
realize that our forever will be with God in heaven.
So we can find strength and perseverance to walk
dusty roads and tread tumultuous waters because
of our faith in Him.

*Dear God, I can't wait to be with You
forever! In Jesus' name I pray. Amen.*

LOVING OTHERS REQUIRES HIS HELP

Remember His call, and live by the royal law found in Scripture: love others as you love yourself. You'll be doing very well if you can get this down.
JAMES 2:8 VOICE

Loving others as you love yourself is a tall order! Mustering desire to show compassion and care for some people is just plain difficult. And while we may want to do the things God asks, this is often the one we push back on the most.

Pray for compassion every day. God is always listening, and He promises to answer you the right way at the right time. Talk to Him about your struggles to love. Tell Him the truth about your resistance. Ask Him to soften your heart and give you courage. There is no shame in admitting you can't do it on your own! God never expected you to.

Dear God, help me follow Your commands to love the unlovable people in my life. I simply cannot do it without Your help. In Jesus' name I pray. Amen.

A GOD-BUILT HOME

We are convinced that even if these bodies we live in are folded up at death like tents, we will still have a God-built home that no human hands have built, which will last forever in the heavenly realm.

2 CORINTHIANS 5:1 TPT

Your faith in Jesus Christ's death and resurrection provides you an eternal home in the heavenly realm. Everything humans put their hands on will wither and die. It will fade into nothing. But no person or thing can take away your forever with the Lord, because it's God who made it possible through Jesus. He is the architect of eternity.

Let your heart be filled with strength and peace, knowing that God has made a way for you to live with Him in heaven forever. Your response to God's calling on your life by placing your faith in Jesus sealed the deal. So ask for courageous faith to make the most of every minute you're here, living to glorify Him before all those around you.

Dear God, thank You for making a way for me to spend eternity with You. I'm excited to live in Your God-built home and praise You forever. In Jesus' name I pray. Amen.

AUTHENTIC FAITH

Brothers and sisters, it doesn't make any sense to say you have faith and act in a way that denies that faith. Mere talk never gets you very far, and a commitment to Jesus only in words will not save you.

JAMES 2:14 VOICE

Ask God to help you be consistent in how you live and who you claim to be. If you declare yourself a follower of the Lord, be purposeful to let that truth shine throughout your life. Don't be all talk and no action. Instead, let your choices prove your faith genuine.

How do you do that? Offer to pray for others when led. Open the Word of God and study it regularly. Make public and private choices that reflect your belief. Walk tall, trusting God in difficult situations rather than living in defeat and fear. Let God authenticate your faith by the fruit that comes from it.

Dear God, I don't want to be a fair-weather follower. I want my faith to be unshakable and undeniable at every turn. Help my belief shine through my words and actions. Prove my faith authentic and genuine. In Jesus' name I pray. Amen.

SHARING THE MESSAGE

We are ambassadors of the Anointed One who carry the message of Christ to the world, as though God were tenderly pleading with them directly through our lips. So we tenderly plead with you on Christ's behalf, "Turn back to God and be reconciled to him."

2 CORINTHIANS 5:20 TPT

Ask God to make you fearless of speaking out so you can be bold about Jesus as you carry His message to the world. You have the privilege and the responsibility of sharing Him with those around you. And when you're courageous to speak truth, God will put the right words in your mouth to share.

Maybe He wants you to unpack your testimony. Maybe someone needs to hear a certain Bible verse as they walk through the dark valley. Maybe a friend needs to know who Jesus is and hear the promise of salvation He brings. In every case, be prayerful so your words are powerful.

Dear God, I'm humbled and honored to share Your awesomeness with others. Open doors and give me words, and I will share Your message. In Jesus' name I pray. Amen.

KNOWING IN YOUR HEART

You can believe all you want that there is one true God, that's wonderful! But even the demons know this and tremble with fear before him, yet they're unchanged—they remain demons.
JAMES 2:19 TPT

Faith is a daily journey that deepens our relationship with God. Some days it feels easy and natural, but other days we struggle to do what we know God has commanded. We have moments when our humanity gets the better of us. So today's verse is the perfect reminder there's a difference between knowing God in your *mind* and knowing God in your *heart*.

As a believer, you should have a craving to learn more about the Lord. You should also have a longing to be in deeper communion with God—a desire for Him to mold you into the woman He intends you to be. Faith should change you from the inside out as you seek Him every day.

Dear God, I don't want to just know about You in my mind. I want to know about You deep in my heart! Give me a continual longing to grow with You! In Jesus' name I pray. Amen.

FAITH AND WORKS

*I can already hear one of you agreeing by
saying, "Sounds good. You take care of the faith
department, I'll handle the works department."
Not so fast. You can no more show me your
works apart from your faith than I can show you
my faith apart from my works. Faith and works,
works and faith, fit together hand in glove.*

JAMES 2:18 MSG

You are saved by faith alone. You didn't earn the gift;
you received it through believing. But through that
faith in the Lord, you will see fruit bloom in your
life. As you become closer to God, your actions will
reveal the authenticity of your faith.

When you love God more, you will be enabled
to love others. When you accept God's grace, you
will have the ability to extend it. When you have
experienced His compassion, you will feel it toward
others. When you focus on God, you will focus less
on yourself, enabling a life of selflessness. Faith and
works fit together in beautiful harmony.

*Dear God, deepen my faith so powerful works
flow from it. In Jesus' name I pray. Amen.*

THE NEED FOR EXPRESSION

And the same is true of the prostitute named Rahab who was found righteous in God's eyes by her works, for she received the spies into her home and helped them escape from the city by another route. For just as a human body without the spirit is a dead corpse, so faith without the expression of good works is dead!

JAMES 2:25–26 TPT

Let this be a challenge to live your faith out loud. Sometimes we hide our faith because those closest to us aren't believers. We may downplay our belief so we don't offend those we care about the most. Or we may cave to societal pressures telling us a life of faith is meaningless.

Want confidence to stand up for what you believe? Ask God for it. Let Him embolden you to speak up. Let Him give you courage to speak out. You should have an internal fire driving you to express faith in your everyday life. Ask God to ignite it and give you strength to stand up.

Dear God, create a fearlessness in me to unabashedly share my faith in meaningful ways. In Jesus' name I pray. Amen.

RUN TO GOD

Trust GOD from the bottom of your heart;
don't try to figure out everything on your own.
Listen for GOD's voice in everything you do,
everywhere you go; he's the one who will keep you
on track. Don't assume that you know it all. Run
to GOD! Run from evil! Your body will glow with
health, your very bones will vibrate with life!
PROVERBS 3:5–8 MSG

If you can walk out today's scripture, your faith will grow. Trusting God over your own abilities will bless you in beautiful and unexpected ways. And you can do that by having a robust prayer life—one in which you seek His voice before you make a move.

The Bible says to run to God for wisdom. Run to Him for strength. Because when we press into the Lord and rely on Him to meet our needs, doing so will benefit us in countless ways. For too long we've just handled things ourselves. We've navigated life our own way. But God will keep us on the right track if we seek Him!

Dear God, I will run to You rather than rest in my own abilities. In Jesus' name I pray. Amen.

COURAGEOUS FAITH

"Did you know that your cousin Elizabeth conceived
a son, old as she is? Everyone called her barren, and
here she is six months pregnant! Nothing, you see,
is impossible with God." And Mary said, Yes, I see it
all now: I'm the Lord's maid, ready to serve. Let it
be with me just as you say. Then the angel left her.
LUKE 1:37–38 MSG

Talk about courage! Young Mary knew the trouble
being pregnant before marriage would cause her.
She knew what it might signal to her soon-to-be
husband. She realized it could bring shame to her
family. But she believed the angel was sent on a
heavenly errand with a message from God, and
that belief settled her heart.

Courageous faith comes from a deep belief and
trust in the Lord. It comes from choosing to believe
that His promises are real and will come to pass.
And it's a deliberate decision to saturate yourself
with prayer so you learn to discern His voice over
everyone else's.

Dear God, help me to be bold in my belief. Bless me
with the faith of Mary. In Jesus' name I pray. Amen.

HIS LOVING CORRECTION

*Honor God with everything you own; give him
the first and the best. Your barns will burst, your
wine vats will brim over. But don't, dear friend,
resent God's discipline; don't sulk under his
loving correction. It's the child he loves that God
corrects; a father's delight is behind all this.*
PROVERBS 3:9–12 MSG

No one likes to be corrected. Nobody enjoys hearing about the things they are doing wrong. But our desire for a strong relationship with our heavenly Father includes receiving His discipline when we're going down the wrong path.

It's important to remember that we will never experience condemnation from God, but we will receive conviction that will lead to repentance. And it's that turning from sin that will deepen our connection to God. Conviction is not to make us feel bad; it is to make us more like Jesus. Through prayer, you will find the courage to receive His loving correction.

*Dear God, my pride keeps me unable to
receive discipline from others. But I know
Your correction comes from a deep well of
love for me, and so I will trust the plans You
have for me. In Jesus' name I pray. Amen.*

BENEFITS OF PRAYER

My message and my preaching weren't
presented with convincing wise words but with
a demonstration of the Spirit and of power. I did
this so that your faith might not depend on the
wisdom of people but on the power of God.
1 CORINTHIANS 2:4–5 CEB

Every moment you spend in prayer benefits you in ways you don't even know. Layers of goodness play out in your life every day that are directly attributed to those sacred moments with God.

Spending time with God softens your heart toward His people. It gives you an eternal perspective on earthly problems. It strengthens your resolve and gives you wisdom for the decisions ahead. It impresses on your heart what to share, how to share, and when to share what He has ordained. And even more, it deepens your connection with the One who created you.

Dear God, I love talking to You in prayer. I'm
thankful that I can tell You anything at any
time. And I'm grateful for the many benefits
that come from this invested time, especially
how Your Holy Spirit prompts me and grows
me in the faith. In Jesus' name I pray. Amen.

TALKING THROUGH ETERNITY

"God so loved the world that he gave his only Son, so that everyone who believes in him won't perish but will have eternal life. God didn't send his Son into the world to judge the world, but that the world might be saved through him."
JOHN 3:16–17 CEB

Because of Jesus, you can have a robust prayer life. His sacrificial death on the cross bridged the gap sin created and made you right in the eyes of God. What an amazing blessing given to the world! What a loving and caring Father to make a way for us to have a relationship with Him.

Start talking to God now, telling Him everything on your heart. He is interested in every detail of your life, from car pool woes to marital strife to tangling insecurities. He wants to know what makes your heart soar and what makes your heart heavy. So invite Him into your life through constant conversation, and let that conversation carry on through to eternity.

Dear God, I'm grateful You made a way for my salvation. I don't ever want to take that for granted. In Jesus' name I pray. Amen.

RUNNING THE RACE

So then, with endurance, let's also run the race
that is laid out in front of us, since we have
such a great cloud of witnesses surrounding
us. Let's throw off any extra baggage, get rid
of the sin that trips us up, and fix our eyes
on Jesus, faith's pioneer and perfecter.
HEBREWS 12:1–2 CEB

The more we spend time in prayer with God, the better we will understand the plans He has determined for our lives. We will find the courage to step out of our comfort zones and pursue His will. We will have endurance, giving us hope and perspective as we walk through our circumstances. And we will be encouraged to give God what's weighing us down so nothing keeps us from focusing on His goodness.

Don't waste a minute trying to figure things out on your own. Go right to God and ask for what you need to persevere. He is the One to straighten our crooked path, restore our faith, and faithfully equip us for the race we've been called to run.

Dear God, help me run the race
with persistence, intentionality, and
faithfulness. In Jesus' name I pray. Amen.

DISCOVERING SATISFACTION

*I know what it means to lack, and I know what it
means to experience overwhelming abundance.
For I'm trained in the secret of overcoming all
things, whether in fullness or in hunger. And
I find that the strength of Christ's explosive
power infuses me to conquer every difficulty.*
PHILIPPIANS 4:12–13 TPT

When you understand that God is your source for
every need, you will find a deep level of contentment. Your faith will grow in leaps and bounds as
you patiently wait for the Lord's provision. And you
will feel a sense of satisfaction that is unattainable
through anything the world has to offer.

The goal is that no matter whether you are experiencing abundance or scarcity, you will recognize
that God is enough. Time spent with Him through
prayer will give you courage to choose faith over
fear. And you will discover satisfaction regardless
of the circumstances surrounding you. They simply
won't have the power to shift your focus from God.

*Dear God, help me understand that You are
all I need. Fill my heart with faith so I do
not waver in my belief based on my life's
situation. In Jesus' name I pray. Amen.*

HE UNDERSTANDS
THE OPPOSITION

So consider carefully how Jesus faced such intense opposition from sinners who opposed their own souls, so that you won't become worn down and cave in under life's pressures.

HEBREWS 12:3 TPT

Without doubt you will face intense pressure throughout your life. Chances are you already have. Calm situations can become messy at a moment's notice. Therefore, your expectations should be grounded in reality.

Consider, then, how blessed we are to have a Savior who understands the complex issues surrounding intense opposition. In Jesus' short life on earth, He experienced the pressures of humanity on every level. That means when we pray about what scares and overwhelms us, He understands. He gets it. Even more, the Lord will give us courage to stand strong and peace and strength to work through the issues we face.

Dear God, You understand firsthand the intense opposition I face. Remind me that You're always ready to help so I don't have to work in my own strength. I need You! In Jesus' name I pray. Amen.

GIVE HIM YOUR ANXIETY

Don't be anxious about anything; rather, bring up all of your requests to God in your prayers and petitions, along with giving thanks. Then the peace of God that exceeds all understanding will keep your hearts and minds safe in Christ Jesus.
PHILIPPIANS 4:6–7 CEB

The best place for you to go when you're apprehensive and stressed out is right to the feet of God. You may try to figure things out on your own. You may look for ways to numb the fear and insecurity. But when you take your worry into the world to look for solutions, you will eventually be let down.

Scripture says that God will give you the kind of peace that makes no sense to those around you. It's a supernatural transaction that calms your anxious heart like nothing else as it emboldens you through faith. And it is available to you every time you ask for it in prayer.

Dear God, my heart is full of worry. I don't feel strong or confident, and I need You to strengthen me. Bless me with Your peace so my anxious heart can be at rest. In Jesus' name I pray. Amen.

EMBRACING CORRECTION

*Fully embrace God's correction as part of your
training, for he is doing what any loving father
does for his children. For who has ever heard
of a child who never had to be corrected?
We all should welcome God's discipline
as the validation of authentic sonship.*

HEBREWS 12:7–8 TPT

What does it look like to fully embrace God's correction? Maybe it means you obey the Holy Spirit's
nudge to rethink your decision. Maybe it means
you're quick to apologize, feeling convicted about
your harsh words. Maybe it means you repent for the
season of sinning you've entertained for too long.

God is the great course corrector, and in doing
so, He's lovingly calling you back. His desire is to
deepen your faith. Ask for courage to return to Him.
In prayer, thank Him for wanting what's best for you.
Thank God for keeping His caring eye upon you.

*Dear God, give me the courage to receive Your
loving examination of my heart for thoughts
and ideas that are not in alignment with Your
will for me. I know You want the very best
for my life. In Jesus' name I pray. Amen.*

WHERE IS YOUR FOCUS?

From now on, brothers and sisters, if anything is excellent and if anything is admirable, focus your thoughts on these things: all that is true, all that is holy, all that is just, all that is pure, all that is lovely, and all that is worthy of praise. Practice these things: whatever you learned, received, heard, or saw in us. The God of peace will be with you.
PHILIPPIANS 4:8–9 CEB

With hardship and heartbreak lapping at your heels daily, take today's scripture to heart. Let it shift your perspective from the problems you're facing to the promises of God. Let it give you courage for the road ahead. Let it be your focus regardless of what you're facing.

You can be bold in your faith if you'll follow what the Bible teaches. If it tells you to focus on things that are excellent and admirable, things that are true and holy and just and pure, doing so will bring a beautiful blessing. Ask God to protect your mind so you can experience the peace of Jesus every day.

Dear God, give me strength to keep my eyes on You. In Jesus' name I pray. Amen.

THE CURE FOR WEAKNESS

*So be made strong even in your weakness
by lifting up your tired hands in prayer and
worship. And strengthen your weak knees, for
as you keep walking forward on God's paths
all your stumbling ways will be divinely healed!*
HEBREWS 12:12–13 TPT

What is the cure for weakness? What can we do when we are feeling hopeless and helpless? Scripture is clear that we'll find strength through our surrender. We will find courage by lifting up our desperate prayers for God's help. We'll receive motivation and perseverance as we acknowledge our lacking. And we will be made confident again as we worship the One who can restore everything, making us wholehearted again.

Let prayer be your first stop. God is always listening, always waiting to hear your voice reach to the heavens. Let your faith be what guides you to the throne of God to ask for His magnificent intervention.

*Dear God, in those times when I feel weak and
incapable, remind me that courage can be found
through You. My weakness can be made strong,
replenished by Your glorious hand. You're what
I need the most. In Jesus' name I pray. Amen.*

THE DOMINO EFFECT OF BLESSINGS

Don't run from tests and hardships, brothers and sisters. As difficult as they are, you will ultimately find joy in them; if you embrace them, your faith will blossom under pressure and teach you true patience as you endure. And true patience brought on by endurance will equip you to complete the long journey and cross the finish line—mature, complete, and wanting nothing.
JAMES 1:2–4 VOICE

God wants you to stand firm in the face of adversity. He wants you to remain steadfast rather than crumble under the pressure that comes from hardship. Why? Because when you do, a domino effect of blessings will result.

When you press into God, you will be able to find joy in those messy moments. Your faith will grow in unexpected ways. Patience and endurance will be new growth in your life. And you will finish well, mature and complete. Make prayer indispensable. It's where you open your heart to God in expectation.

Dear God, I want to stand firm, courageous because of You! In Jesus' name I pray. Amen.

CRISIS OF FAITH

Jesus said to [the father of the demon-possessed boy], "What do you mean 'if'? If you are able to believe, all things are possible to the believer." When he heard this, the boy's father cried out with tears, saying, "I do believe, Lord; help my little faith!" Now when Jesus saw that the crowd was quickly growing larger, he commanded the demon, saying, "Deaf and mute spirit, I command you to come out of him and never enter him again!"
MARK 9:23–25 TPT

Sometimes we need help with our faith because we're struggling to believe what we know is true. Don't beat yourself up over that; it's a common challenge. We believe the Bible but worry that God won't show up for us in the same way as our favorite characters. We're certain of His goodness but feel unworthy. Or we trust in His sovereignty but feel overlooked.

Every time you have a crisis of faith, pray. Be honest. Tell God about it and ask for help. He's not expecting perfection from you, just authenticity. Let Him be the One to encourage your belief and strengthen it.

*Dear God, I believe. Help my unbelief.
In Jesus' name I pray. Amen.*

ASK FOR WHAT YOU NEED

*If you don't have all the wisdom needed for
this journey, then all you have to do is ask God
for it; and God will grant all that you need.
He gives lavishly and never scolds you for asking.*
JAMES 1:5 VOICE

How amazing is that? You can ask God for what you need, and He will provide it. Scripture confirms it, saying that God will grant all that you need. Even more, He will give it lavishly and without rebuke.

If you need wisdom, ask God. If you need a dose of courage, ask. Do you need compassion or generosity? Do you lack peace or joy? Maybe you're in need of financial provision. Maybe you're looking for a miracle cure for a scary diagnosis. Do you need patience? Endurance? Maybe you need a shift in perspective or the ability to forgive. Go to your Father in prayer and ask, believing He will grant all that you need.

*Dear God, thank You for meeting my needs.
I'm so grateful for Your generosity and kindness!
I love You. In Jesus' name I pray. Amen.*

GROWING FAITH

*Then the disciples came to Jesus in private and said,
"Why couldn't we throw the demon out?" "Because
you have little faith," he said. "I assure you that if
you have faith the size of a mustard seed, you could
say to this mountain, 'Go from here to there,' and
it will go. There will be nothing that you can't do."*
MATTHEW 17:19–20 CEB

How do you grow your faith? The truth is the more
time you spend with God, your faith will increase.
Every prayer you pray matters. Every time you
cry out for help, it counts. Whenever you choose
to trust God rather than allow fear to tangle you,
you will grow.

Having faith means you believe that God is who
He says He is and that He will do what He says He
will do. Sometimes faith flows through us with ease,
but other times it takes true grit. Ask the Lord to
mature your faith every day so that when you need
it most it's available.

*Dear God, help me become a strong and
sturdy woman of faith who believes no
matter what. In Jesus' name I pray. Amen.*

BEAUTIFUL BLESSINGS

If your faith remains strong, even while surrounded by life's difficulties, you will continue to experience the untold blessings of God! True happiness comes as you pass the test with faith, and receive the victorious crown of life promised to every lover of God!

JAMES 1:12 TPT

Sometimes we want to crumble under the pressure. We want to jump into bed and pull the covers over our head, hiding away from the mess. When life throws a curveball, it often weakens our knees and tests our resolve. But be encouraged to know that beautiful blessings come from strengthening yourself in the Lord.

Every time you cry out to the Lord, He hears you. He understands the complexity of emotions you are battling. And He is ready to strengthen you in the battle, building your courage to remain strong through every difficulty. Friend, let the Lord meet your needs and bless you for asking.

Dear God, help me to have confidence in You. Let me be quick to pray for Your support as I navigate life's difficulties. And thank You for blessing my obedience. In Jesus' name I pray. Amen.

YOU DON'T NEED MORE

*The apostles came up and said to the Master,
"Give us more faith." But the Master said, "You
don't need more faith. There is no 'more' or 'less'
in faith. If you have a bare kernel of faith, say the
size of a poppy seed, you could say to this sycamore
tree, 'Go jump in the lake,' and it would do it."*
LUKE 17:5–6 MSG

As women, we often strive for more. We want our
marriage to be stronger and our parenting to be
unmatched. We want to look ten years younger
and our fitness level to reflect the same. And we
want top recognition at our job, to be praised for
our culinary skills, and others to envy the beauty of
our home. But more isn't always better.

God says we don't need more faith. We just
need to trust and believe in the power it affords
us. And the time we spend in His Word and in His
presence through prayer makes that happen. It's
what creates courageous faith.

*Dear God, deepen the faith I have so I'm not
striving for more. In Jesus' name I pray. Amen.*

LISTEN FIRST

My dearest brothers and sisters, take this to heart:
Be quick to listen, but slow to speak. And be slow
to become angry, for human anger is never a
legitimate tool to promote God's righteous purpose.
JAMES 1:19–20 TPT

Keeping our mouth shut so that we can listen takes courage and strength, especially when we feel the need to defend ourselves. It's not easy to bite our tongue as we allow someone to unpack what they're feeling when we think they're off base. Why might the Lord ask us to be slow to speak and quick to listen?

These are the moments when our anger can spill out, causing us to sin against both the one sharing their heart and God. The last thing we want to do is say something we can't take back. While it may feel good in the moment, we don't want to cause harm. When you find yourself in this situation again, pray immediately and ask for the courage to stay silent and listen.

Dear God, give me patience to hear before
I speak. Help me demonstrate love and
compassion. In Jesus' name I pray. Amen.

CRUCIFIED WITH CHRIST

Indeed, I have been crucified with Christ. My ego is no longer central. It is no longer important that I appear righteous before you or have your good opinion, and I am no longer driven to impress God. Christ lives in me. The life you see me living is not "mine," but it is lived by faith in the Son of God, who loved me and gave himself for me. I am not going to go back on that.
GALATIANS 2:20–21 MSG

Consider the perspective shift Paul was describing in this passage. If your desire is to deepen your relationship with the Lord, let this be how you think. Not only is it a faithful mindset, but it's also a courageous one.

Paul understood that being *crucified with Christ* meant his life took a backseat because Jesus was now the driver. He had surrendered to faith, letting the opinions and comforts of the world fall away. When we follow Paul's example, we'll create unshakable faith that will carry us through every difficulty life brings our way.

Dear God, help my life reflect my steadfast faith in You and surrender to You. In Jesus' name I pray. Amen.

DON'T JUST HEAR IT

Don't just listen to the Word of Truth and not respond to it, for that is the essence of self-deception. So always let his Word become like poetry written and fulfilled by your life!
JAMES 1:22 TPT

Be the kind of faith-filled woman who not only hears the Word but acts on it. Boldly respond with fervor. The world is already full of people who don't follow through. We know talk is cheap. And we're saturated with those who have good intentions. Friend, be different.

Every day, ask God to help you walk out your faith with great intentionality. Pray that your time in the Word proves fruitful by the decisions you make. Be courageous as you choose what you know pleases God over what may satisfy your flesh. Let His will be what drives every part of your life, and watch as your relationship with the Lord finds firm footing.

Dear God, I don't want just to hear Your Word and do nothing about it. Make me bold enough to choose Your will and ways every day, even when it's the difficult choice. In Jesus' name I pray. Amen.

UNAPOLOGETICALLY COMMITTED

And now the time is fast approaching for my release from this life and I am ready to be offered as a sacrifice. I have fought an excellent fight. I have finished my full course with all my might and I've kept my heart full of faith.

2 TIMOTHY 4:6–7 TPT

What a courageous mindset! No doubt Paul acquired it through time spent with God. We aren't born thinking so courageously and sacrificially. This mindset was earned through an unshakable relationship with the Lord. Paul lived unapologetically committed to following God's plan for his life. He boldly proclaimed truth and was unafraid of any natural consequences doing so brought his way.

There's something beautiful and powerful about staying the course no matter what. Standing up for the right thing is often the hard thing to do, but it points directly to your faith. And living this way requires God's strength and perseverance. Don't be shy to ask Him for it.

Dear God, make me a bold witness for You. I want to be unapologetically committed to sharing Your goodness in the world. In Jesus' name I pray. Amen.

DO THEY LINE UP?

If someone believes they have a relationship with God but fails to guard his words then his heart is drifting away and his religion is shallow and empty.

JAMES 1:26 TPT

Let this warning cause you to take inventory of your faith, making sure it's authentic and real. Our words and actions must line up with what we believe, or the discrepancy should cause us to rethink our commitment. If they don't mirror each other, we should question the validity.

If we say we love God but treat others terribly, do we really love Him? If we can't forgive others or we choose to use words as weapons, are we full of faith? Are we a saint on Sunday and a terror the rest of the week? Friend, dig in deep with the Lord through prayer, asking Him to prove your faith authentic. Ask Him to make you courageous as you pursue righteousness.

Dear God, I don't want to only believe I have a good relationship with You; I want to know it! I want my faith to be authentic and above reproach. Help my pursuit. In Jesus' name I pray. Amen.

NO MATTER WHAT

Proclaim the Word of God and stand upon it no matter what! Rise to the occasion and preach when it is convenient and when it is not. Preach in the full expression of the Holy Spirit—with wisdom and patience as you instruct and teach the people.
2 TIMOTHY 4:2 TPT

If you are waiting for things to slow down before you step into the will of God, it will never happen. If you feel inconvenienced by His prompting and justify your way out of action, you're missing the point. God wants you to be bold in your faith, willing to rise to the occasion as it presents itself.

Keep open communication with the Lord and let Him be the One who guides your day. Be sensitive to His leading and willing to step up and speak out in a moment's notice. Because He is trustworthy, you can follow God's direction with courage and confidence, knowing you are always safe in His will.

Dear God, You are never an inconvenience! I am blessed to be called a child of God, and I will follow You anywhere! In Jesus' name I pray. Amen.

BEING A LIGHT TO THE LOST

For the time is coming when they will no longer listen and respond to the healing words of truth because they will become selfish and proud. They will seek out teachers with soothing words that line up with their desires, saying just what they want to hear. They will close their ears to the truth and believe nothing but fables and myths.
2 TIMOTHY 4:3–4 TPT

We must have courageous faith now, for many think the time mentioned in this passage of scripture is already here. If you look around, you can certainly see evidence of it. So how can we ensure we don't fall prey? By being intentional to create a stronger connection to our heavenly Father through prayer, the result being a bold belief and resolve.

Ask God for wisdom and discernment. Ask for a confident faith. Ask the Lord to make you fearless to share His Word and your testimony of His goodness. Choose to be a light to the lost.

Dear God, give me courage to be a truth teller and a light to those who need to know You. In Jesus' name I pray. Amen.

BLESSING OBEDIENCE

You see, to love God means that we keep His commands, and His commands don't weigh us down. Everything that has been fathered by God overcomes the corrupt world. This is the victory that has conquered the world: our faith.
1 JOHN 5:3–4 VOICE

Obedience is important to the Lord, which is probably why He mentions countless times in His Word that He will bless it. Friend, keeping God's commands is a privilege. To look at it any other way is dangerous. Even more, what God asks of us should never be considered a burden. It shouldn't weigh us down, because His requests will never be heavier than the grace provided for them.

Let this truth motivate and encourage you to spend solid time with God. Doing so will transform your heart so it aligns with His will, giving you the courage to let Him be the Leader of your life. And it will create in you an excitement to be His hands and feet to the world.

Dear God, I love You and am committed to keeping Your commands, knowing Your yoke is light. In Jesus' name I pray. Amen.

ONLY POSSIBLE WITH GOD

*But for right now, until that completeness,
we have three things to do to lead us toward
that consummation: Trust steadily in God,
hope unswervingly, love extravagantly.
And the best of the three is love.*
1 CORINTHIANS 13:13 MSG

Walking out today's verse is possible only with God's help. It requires His grace flowing through you, and it's not something you're able to do in your own strength—at least not for long. Therefore a strong relationship with God is vital to living a faithful life.

When you invest time in the Lord, in His Word, and in His people, you'll find courage and confidence to trust fearlessly. You'll have hope that's unshakable. And you will love lavishly even those who make doing so difficult. Don't skimp on your prayer life! Let it be an essential part of every day.

*Dear God, the Word is very clear about Your
desire for our lives. Not only do I want to glorify
Your name in all that I do, but I also want to
point others to You with my life. Help me to be a
beacon of hope. In Jesus' name I pray. Amen.*

ASKING FOR WHAT FITS

We live in the bold confidence that God hears our voices when we ask for things that fit His plan. And if we have no doubt that He hears our voices, we can be assured that He moves in response to our call.
1 John 5:14–15 voice

What a good reminder that God hears us when we pray. More specifically, He hears our requests for things that fit His plan. Sure, we can ask for the new car, a job promotion, overnight weight loss, or a new puppy, but scripture says we can have *bold confidence* that our requests reach God's throne room when we ask according to His will.

How do you know you're asking for things that fit God's plan? Let the Bible be a reference guide. Use prayer time to listen for His voice. Look for confirmation from scripture, sermons, or advice from a trusted friend. Girl, go before the throne fearlessly, trusting God to answer in ways that glorify Him and benefit you.

Dear God, I'm grateful I can ask You for anything at any time. Help me trust that Your answers are always the right ones. In Jesus' name I pray. Amen.

WHAT IS LOVE?

Love is patient, love is kind, it isn't jealous, it doesn't brag, it isn't arrogant, it isn't rude, it doesn't seek its own advantage, it isn't irritable, it doesn't keep a record of complaints, it isn't happy with injustice, but it is happy with the truth. Love puts up with all things, trusts in all things, hopes for all things, endures all things.
1 CORINTHIANS 13:4–7 CEB

What a beautiful definition of God's love we find in 1 Corinthians 13. Think about how much better the world would be if this is how we chose to interact with one another. We would be better spouses, better parents, better siblings, better neighbors, and better friends. But the truth is that living this way requires courage, strength, and grace. This is not an easy task, and so often we get it wrong.

The only chance you have at showing love in this manner is through God's help. Every day, before your feet hit the floor, ask God to love the world *through* you. Let Him fill you with a bold resolve to prioritize others selflessly.

Dear God, I simply cannot love well without You, for You are love. In Jesus' name I pray. Amen.

HOW DO YOU MEASURE YOUR WORTH?

God has given me grace to speak a warning about pride. I would ask each of you to be emptied of self-promotion and not create a false image of your importance. Instead, honestly assess your worth by using your God-given faith as the standard of measurement, and then you will see your true value with an appropriate self-esteem.
ROMANS 12:3 TPT

If we choose to find our value in what the world says is important, we will never find joy. If we're obsessed with receiving approval from those around us, we will always feel lacking. Every time we measure ourselves against an earthly standard, we will come out with the short end of the stick. Rather than feel courageous and strong, we will feel weak and unworthy.

Let the Lord speak your true value into your spirit based on your faith. Go to Him in prayer and ask God to reveal how He sees you. You'll be delighted by what you discover.

Dear God, give me a true assessment of my worth according to Your standard of measurement of my value. In Jesus' name I pray. Amen.

HOLDING FIRMLY

Remember to stay alert and hold firmly to all that you believe. Be mighty and full of courage. Let love and kindness be the motivation behind all that you do.
1 CORINTHIANS 16:13–14 TPT

Sometimes the world feels crazy. We see things happening that we can't explain, and they worry us. We watch troubling trends come and go. And we are forced to navigate relationship struggles, financial strains, and worrisome health challenges. How can those things not shake us to the core?

But once again, God's Word gives us the key to maintaining a peaceful heart in the midst of this wacky world: faith. We're told to hold firmly to what we believe. Why? Because it's exactly what will keep us confident in God. Faith will embolden us to stand strong. And faith will be what softens our heart with compassion so the ebbs and flows of the world won't harden it.

Dear God, help me grow closer to You so I'm stabilized when the world feels out of control. Give me courage. Make me bold. And let love be my motivation. In Jesus' name I pray. Amen.

THE IMITATION GAME

Stop imitating the ideals and opinions of the culture around you, but be inwardly transformed by the Holy Spirit through a total reformation of how you think. This will empower you to discern God's will as you live a beautiful life, satisfying and perfect in his eyes.

ROMANS 12:2 TPT

Ask God to retrain your brain. Let Him be the One to transform your stinkin' thinkin' so it doesn't guide your actions. Sometimes, without realizing it, we fall prey to the ideals and opinions of the culture we live in. Every day we are bombarded with their standards, and it's no wonder we begin to imitate what we see. But that doesn't glorify the Lord.

When you ask, God will give you discernment. He will open your eyes to the places in your heart that need addressing. And He will give you courage to make the necessary changes so you can stand your ground in faith. The result will be contentment as you feel God's delight.

Dear God, I don't want to play the imitation game. I want a transformed mind that focuses on a beautiful life with You. In Jesus' name I pray. Amen.

PRAY WITH CONFIDENCE

*Jesus said, "What can I do for you?" The blind
man said, "Rabbi, I want to see." "On your
way," said Jesus. "Your faith has saved and
healed you." In that very instant he recovered
his sight and followed Jesus down the road.*
MARK 10:51–52 MSG

The blind man did not mince words. He didn't beat
around the bush. Jesus didn't have to decipher what
he was asking for. No, this man spoke boldly and
clearly, asking the Lord for a miracle. In his desperation, the blind man asked without hesitation.

Friend, God wants you to approach Him in
prayer with confidence. He wants you to pray with
a hopeful attitude and to be open and honest about
what you need. You won't be mocked. You won't be
shamed. You won't be rejected. Courageously tell
God what is on your heart, trusting He will respond
at the perfect time and in ways that benefit you
and glorify Him.

*Dear God, thank You for caring so deeply
about me. Thank You for the freedom to ask
for what I want. And thank You for answering
with what I need. In Jesus' name I pray. Amen.*

COURAGEOUS KIND OF LOVE

*Let the inner movement of your heart always
be to love one another, and never play the role
of an actor wearing a mask. Despise evil and
embrace everything that is good and virtuous.
Be devoted to tenderly loving your fellow
believers as members of one family. Try to outdo
yourselves in respect and honor of one another.*
ROMANS 12:9–10 TPT

The greatest command is to love God, and the
second greatest is to love others. Nothing is more
important to God. As a matter of fact, He desires
for love to operate out of the depths of our heart.
It should be an integral part of who we are and how
we move, causing us to despise evil and embrace
what is good. It should cause us to be devoted and
tender toward others. The problem is we are unable
to make this happen in our humanity.

Ask God to let love reign in your heart. Ask
for the courageous kind of love that mirrors His
compassion. And then let it flow through you to
bless others.

*Dear God, I can only love this way with Your help.
Fill my heart. In Jesus' name I pray. Amen.*

WE'RE TO BE STILL

*"Be still, be calm, see, and understand I am the
True God. I am honored among all the nations.
I am honored over all the earth." You know the
Eternal, the Commander of heavenly armies,
surrounds us and protects us; the True God
of Jacob is our shelter, close to His heart.*

PSALM 46:10–11 VOICE

When life throws a curveball, many of us freak out.
It rocks the core of our sense of security, and we
are deeply shaken. We look down the road and see
nothing but horrible outcomes and endings as our
minds go into overdrive. And we often get busy
trying to fix things ourselves. We aren't trusting
the Lord; we are in "go mode."

Let this kind of response be a red flag to take
a step back. God wants us to know He is in control.
We're to be courageous in faith as we become still
in His presence. So ask God for a sense of calm and
a deeper understanding of who He is.

*Dear God, I'm not good at being still.
Help me find the grit to surrender to Your
sovereignty. In Jesus' name I pray. Amen.*

WHEN FAITH NEEDS A JOLT

*Be enthusiastic to serve the Lord, keeping
your passion toward him boiling hot! Radiate
with the glow of the Holy Spirit and let him
fill you with excitement as you serve him.
Let this hope burst forth within you, releasing
a continual joy. Don't give up in a time of
trouble, but commune with God at all times.*
ROMANS 12:11–12 TPT

Are you bored with the work you do for the Lord?
Are you uninspired in your relationship with Him?
Is your prayer life unengaging? If these are true,
let prayer be your next step. Ask Him to infuse you
with enthusiasm and excitement. Ask for a renewal
of hope and joy! Be bold in your request to spice
up your faith journey.

When praying for things that align with God's
will, be confident you'll receive them. With His help,
your passion will be reignited with fervor. Courage
will arise for sharing your testimony with others.
And you'll have a resolve to stand strong, even in
the most troubling times.

*Dear God, reinvigorate my faith so I
am more effective for Your kingdom!
In Jesus' name I pray. Amen.*

GOD IS NEARER

*God is our shelter and our strength. When troubles
seem near, God is nearer, and He's ready to help.
So why run and hide? No fear, no pacing, no biting
fingernails. When the earth spins out of control,
we are sure and fearless. When mountains crumble
and the waters run wild, we are sure and fearless.*
PSALM 46:1–2 VOICE

Let these powerful words wash over you today: *God
is nearer.* Grab on to them and hold tight because
they will sustain you when life gets hard. No matter
what fears are closing in on you, God is nearer.
Regardless of the insecurities shutting you down,
the Lord is even closer. No matter what trial comes
your way, God is with you.

Take heart and have courage knowing nothing
can come between you and the Lord. Nothing. And
He is always ready to intervene on your behalf, so
there is no reason to worry. It's a wasted emotion.
God is your shelter and strength, so rest in Him.

*Dear God, what a relief to know You are
nearer than anything else and always
will be. In Jesus' name I pray. Amen.*

KEEPING PRIDE AT BAY

*Live happily together in a spirit of harmony,
and be as mindful of another's worth as you
are your own. Don't live with a lofty mind-set,
thinking you are too important to serve others,
but be willing to do menial tasks and identify with
those who are humble minded. Don't be smug or
even think for a moment that you know it all.*

ROMANS 12:16 TPT

Pride is a destructive mindset. It's in the opposite direction of God's desire for your life, and it will do nothing but alienate you from any meaningful community. He wants us to be harmonious, operating with a servant's attitude.

You can be courageous without being arrogant. You can be bold in your faith without being smug. Ask God to keep your heart pure so it is untainted by conceit. Ask Him to establish in you a heart of humility, because that is what delights Him.

*Dear God, help me pursue harmony in my
relationships. Let me see others as equal.
And keep me humble so I can glorify You
in all I do. In Jesus' name I pray. Amen.*

GOD IS YOUR SOURCE

I pray that God, the source of all hope, will infuse your lives with an abundance of joy and peace in the midst of your faith so that your hope will overflow through the power of the Holy Spirit.
ROMANS 15:13 VOICE

God is the source for all you need. Let that truth sink deep into your DNA today because understanding it will change everything. Do you need hope? Ask God for it. Do you need joy? He will provide it. Are you in need of peace? God will give it to you. Scripture says He is the One who will infuse our lives with what we need.

Ask God to deepen your relationship with Him so you will have a better understanding of who He is and what He promises for believers. Spend time in prayer, asking for a fresh revelation of His goodness. And let Him be the sustainer of your heart so you can experience courageous faith.

Dear God, infuse my life with abundance. I want more of You, more faith, more courage, and more hope. I know You are my source. In Jesus' name I pray. Amen.

VENGEANCE IS GOD'S ALONE

Beloved, don't be obsessed with taking revenge, but leave that to God's righteous justice. For the Scriptures say: "Vengeance is mine, and I will repay," says the Lord. And: If your enemy is hungry, buy him lunch! Win him over with kindness. For your surprising generosity will awaken his conscience, and God will reward you with favor. Never let evil defeat you, but defeat evil with good.
ROMANS 12:19–21 TPT

Ask God to make you bold in your belief that vengeance is His. We need to believe big; otherwise we will take matters into our own hands. But scripture is clear when it says that revenge is not ours. Instead, the Lord tells us to have surprising generosity and kindness toward our enemies.

Ask God to make this truth a powerful force in your life. Ask Him to embolden your faith in His sovereignty. And remember to stand strong, committed to doing good to everyone.

Dear God, replace my vengeful heart with compassion, even for those who hurt me. Help me trust that You will make things right in Your way and in Your timing. In Jesus' name I pray. Amen.

BECOMING HIS FOLLOWER

This gospel unveils a continual revelation of God's righteousness—a perfect righteousness given to us when we believe. And it moves us from receiving life through faith, to the power of living by faith. This is what the Scripture means when it says: "We are right with God through life-giving faith!"

ROMANS 1:17 TPT

When you become a follower of Jesus and make a commitment to Him being the leader of your life, you receive His righteousness. Simply stated, you're in a right relationship with God. Jesus' death on the cross washed away your sins, making you clean in the eyes of the Father. Even more, it affords you access to His power in your life.

Have you asked the Lord to be your Savior? Have you repented of your sins? If not, here is your prayer. . .

Dear God, I boldly confess I'm a sinner in need of a Savior. I'm choosing to follow You, believing the blood of Jesus has justified me in Your eyes. I believe He is Your one and only Son, who lived a perfect life and was crucified to take the punishment for my sins. He rose from the tomb three days later, conquering death. Today I commit my life to You. In Jesus' name I pray. Amen.

THE FEARLESSNESS OF PAUL

I refuse to be ashamed of the wonderful message of God's liberating power unleashed in us through Christ! For I am thrilled to preach that everyone who believes is saved— the Jew first, and then people everywhere!
ROMANS 1:16 TPT

No one would argue that Paul was a fearless follower of God. Once he became a believer, his ministry was unstoppable. The Lord infused him with a courageous faith that made Paul unafraid to speak truth to anyone who would listen. Wherever God sent him to speak, Paul obeyed.

Are you embarrassed to share your story with others? Do you keep your faith to yourself, afraid of being judged or criticized? If so, ask God to give you the fearlessness of Paul. Pray for a courageousness to tell those around you about how the Lord has worked in your life. Trust that He will bolster your bravery at the right time.

Dear God, I do not want to be ashamed of the Gospel in any way. Give me the grit to speak up every time the opportunity presents itself. Make me bold! In Jesus' name I pray. Amen.

DON'T BE GIVEN OVER

*So God abandoned them to their hearts'
desires, which led to the moral corruption of
degrading their own bodies with each other.
They traded God's truth for a lie, and they
worshipped and served the creation instead
of the creator, who is blessed forever. Amen.*
ROMANS 1:24–25 CEB

Passages of scripture like today's should startle you awake. The truth is that at some point, God will give people over to the desires of their heart. That's why it's so important that we stay connected—deeply connected—to our wonderful Father in heaven. That's why we need to dig into His Word and spend time in prayer, growing our relationship and learning more about Him. That's why we must follow His commands as best as possible.

Reconnect with God today. Tell Him again of your commitment to following His will and ways. Let God know what He means to you. And ask for courage to stand strong in your faith in this crazy world.

Dear God, today's verses are sobering. Keep me close to Your heart, Father, convicting me if I stray too far from Your will. In Jesus' name I pray. Amen.

WHY YOU ARE RIGHTEOUS

We know that no one receives God's perfect
righteousness as a reward for keeping the
law, but only by the faith of Jesus, the
Messiah! His faithfulness has saved us, and
we have received God's perfect righteousness.
Now we know that God accepts no one
by the keeping of religious laws!
GALATIANS 2:16 TPT

We're righteous in the eyes of God because of
His faithfulness. It's not something we did. It's not
something we're currently doing. It's not the hope
of something we might do in the future. It has
nothing to do with keeping the law or following pro-
tocol. We're not righteous because of our lineage
or because we have a family member in ministry.
It's not up to us. Instead, it's all because of Jesus.

When you accept Jesus as your Savior, you're
welcomed into the family of believers. His blood
shed on the cross removed your sins, so God sees
you as righteous. And because you cannot earn
salvation or lose it, live with courageous faith so
your life reflects the awesome power of the Lord.

Dear God, You made me righteous!
In Jesus' name I pray. Amen.

UNABLE TO DERAIL YOU

*Although they are fully aware of God's laws and
proper order, and knowing that those who do all
of these things deserve to die, yet they still go
headlong into darkness, encouraging others to do
the same and applauding them when they do!*
ROMANS 1:32 TPT

Have the courage to stand up for what you know is
right. Courageous faith delights the heart of God
and keeps you in a right relationship with Him. As
you know from firsthand experience, countless
forces are trying to derail your faith. The world
has no shortage of ill intentions designed to lead
you into darkness. That's why it's vital you cling to
the Lord.

Ask God to make you bold to stand your ground.
Ask for an extra measure of confidence to follow
His way, even when there is blowback. And when
you feel the temptation to give in, ask the Lord to
make you brave as you choose wisely.

*Dear God, help me to be strong in my
convictions when the world tries to sway me.
Let me not waver in my pursuit of righteous
living. In Jesus' name I pray. Amen.*

WRAPPING YOURSELF IN FAITH

In every battle, take faith as your wrap-around shield, for it is able to extinguish the blazing arrows coming at you from the evil one! Embrace the power of salvation's full deliverance, like a helmet to protect your thoughts from lies. And take the mighty razor-sharp Spirit-sword of the spoken word of God.
EPHESIANS 6:16–18 TPT

Wrap yourself in faith when you feel the walls begin to close in on you. When you discern trouble coming your way, run into the arms of the Lord. When you feel targeted by the enemy, cry out to God. Let your faith in His promises be what strengthens you for the battle ahead.

Scripture promises that we will have hard times in this life. Our faith does not reroute us from facing difficulties. But we can build an unshakable faith through time in God's presence. We can build a strong foundation of trust by recalling times of answered prayer. And God will use our faith to extinguish the arrows meant for our destruction.

Dear God, strengthen my faith.
In Jesus' name I pray. Amen.

SURE OF YOUR SALVATION

So if you believe deep in your heart that God raised Jesus from the pit of death and if you voice your allegiance by confessing the truth that "Jesus is Lord," then you will be saved! Belief begins in the heart and leads to a life that's right with God; confession departs from our lips and brings eternal salvation.

ROMANS 10:9–10 VOICE

It is possible to live in confidence of your salvation. You don't have to worry or wonder if your eternity is secure with God. Scripture is very clear on this subject, helping you settle the matter of your salvation once and for all.

When you have faith that Jesus was raised from the dead by the Father and you publicly declare your unwavering belief that Jesus is Lord, it is settled. Even more, that belief will be revealed through your actions. All will see the visible and tangible proof of your choice to follow Christ.

Dear God, I have believing faith according to what scripture says. Build confidence in me so I no longer question my salvation. In Jesus' name I pray. Amen.

SUPERNATURAL TRANSACTION

Now my beloved ones, I have saved these most important truths for last: Be supernaturally infused with strength through your life-union with the Lord Jesus. Stand victorious with the force of his explosive power flowing in and through you.

EPHESIANS 6:10 TPT

What a blessing to know you don't have to handle everything on your own. Your freedom is not up to you alone. You don't have to muster the courage or the wisdom or the strength. Instead, you can receive it in a supernatural transaction because of your faith.

When you activate your faith in the Lord— trusting Him in all things—you'll be infused with what you need in that moment. Hope? Courage? Discernment? Endurance? Yes, the Holy Spirit's *explosive power* will flow through you as you navigate the challenging circumstances life has brought your way. And it will deliver you a much-needed victory because you stand strong in faith.

Dear God, what a blessing to know You will be with me every step of the way. Thank You for honoring my faith through supernatural transactions. I trust You, I believe in You, and I love You. In Jesus' name I pray. Amen.

THE COURAGE TO SHARE

*And [Jesus] said to them, "As you go into all
the world, preach openly the wonderful news
of the gospel to the entire human race!"*
MARK 16:15 TPT

Sharing your faith with others takes courage. You
may feel confident to talk with your family or close
friends, but it takes grit to open up to those you
don't know. Nevertheless, God's plan is for us to
be open and authentic about our story, exercising
modest honesty when necessary.

Talk to God about your fears surrounding sharing your faith. Let Him know what insecurities are
screaming at you. He is the One who can make you
courageous so you can speak up. He will give you
the assurances necessary to let down your guard.
And you can trust that God will bless you for obeying His command to share the news throughout
the world. He won't set you up for failure. He will
reward your bravery.

*Dear God, help me to be bold as I tell
others about Your goodness. And let me
be more concerned about obeying You
than about any negative reaction I might
receive. In Jesus' name I pray. Amen.*

THE ARMOR WE NEED

*Put on God's complete set of armor provided
for us, so that you will be protected as you fight
against the evil strategies of the accuser! Your
hand-to-hand combat is not with human beings,
but with the highest principalities and authorities
operating in rebellion under the heavenly realms.
For they are a powerful class of demon-gods and
evil spirits that hold this dark world in bondage.*
EPHESIANS 6:11–12 TPT

Let's not forget that our heartache and discouragement are assignments from the enemy. The pain may
come because an important relationship ended in
betrayal. The hurt may stem from a rude comment.
Our frustration may be fueled by the actions of a
neighbor or a coworker. The letdown may come from
our child's decision. But it's important we remember
that our battle is not with human beings, but instead
with demonic principalities and authorities.

Only God gives you courageous faith to discern the difference and take the next right step.
And choosing to put on His armor through prayer
as described in Ephesians 6 strengthens you for
every battle.

*Dear God, remind me to put on Your armor
every day. In Jesus' name I pray. Amen.*

LIVING SELFISHLY

*"Look at that man, bloated by self-importance—
full of himself but soul-empty. But the person
in right standing before God through loyal and
steady believing is fully alive, really alive."*

HABAKKUK 2:4 MSG

Sometimes we inflate our value. We become wise
in our own eyes, thinking we are better than others.
And when we do this, not only do we alienate ourselves from others, but we alienate ourselves from
God. It's not that He has walked away from us; it's
that we feel He's an unnecessary part of our lives.

We will experience life in beautiful ways by
understanding our position in relation to God's
position. When we recognize this truth, it will cause
us to live righteously rather than selfishly. And we
will find the resolve to have believing faith in all
that we do, focused on serving God with fervor.

*Dear God, I confess the times I have been selfish
in my words and thoughts and actions. I have
been bloated by self-importance. Thank You for
the gift of forgiveness through Your Son. From
today forward, help me focus on my faith more
than anything else. In Jesus' name I pray. Amen.*

HUNGRY OR THIRSTY?

Jesus said to them, "I am the Bread of Life. Come every day to me and you will never be hungry. Believe in me and you will never be thirsty."
JOHN 6:35 TPT

Every day we need Jesus. We need His comfort when our hearts are heavy. We need His wisdom when we don't know what to do next. We need His strength when we feel weak and overwhelmed. Every day the invitation stands for you to take those places of lack to the One who gives in abundance.

Scripture is clear that when we go to the Lord in need, we will find satisfaction. His plan has always been to support those who love Him. And when we need refreshment, we can approach the throne in belief, certain we will find it. Let these truths embolden you to be honest with God about your hardships. You will not leave unheard or unfulfilled.

Dear God, You are the Bread that satisfies. You are the One who meets every spoken and unspoken need. I know I can come to You and bare my soul, always expectant for Your goodness. In Jesus' name I pray. Amen.

WHERE IS YOUR INVESTMENT?

The love of money is the root of all kinds of evil. Some have wandered away from the faith and have impaled themselves with a lot of pain because they made money their goal. But as for you, man of God, run away from all these things. Instead, pursue righteousness, holy living, faithfulness, love, endurance, and gentleness.
1 TIMOTHY 6:10–11 CEB

What are the things you pursue? Being known? Having stuff? Getting ahead? Buying more? Today's scripture warns that when we invest in the unhealthy love of money, it opens the door to evil. It's at the very root. And the directive from this passage is to run in the other direction if our passion for cash becomes the goal of life.

It takes courage to walk away from what this world offers. But God will help you invest in the right things, like righteousness and holy living. He will give you the ability to seek love and endurance and gentleness. Let your prayer time be filled with these requests!

Dear God, help me to be bold in my pursuit of righteous living. In Jesus' name I pray. Amen.

GOD'S AGENDA

All that My Father gives to Me comes to Me.
I will receive everyone; I will not send away
anyone who comes to Me. And here's the reason:
I have come down from heaven not to pursue
My own agenda but to do what He desires. I am
here on behalf of the Father who sent Me.
JOHN 6:37–38 VOICE

Jesus knew His mission. He understood the stakes and knew the Father's will. Jesus knew why this was an important step in history. So He kept His eye focused on following God's plan instead of pursuing any plan of His own.

Truth is, it's not easy to turn from our own agenda to God's will. But when He determined your calling, He also secured the details surrounding it. That means you can be confident that if God has asked you to be a writer or speaker, the words will come. If His plan is for you to be a missionary, you'll have the financial support. Ask God to give you courageous faith to do His work.

Dear God, I'm here to walk out Your will—not mine—for my life. In Jesus' name I pray. Amen.

FIGHTING WITH FAITH

*So fight with faith for the winner's prize! Lay
your hands upon eternal life, to which you were
called and about which you made the good
confession before the multitude of witnesses!*

1 TIMOTHY 6:12 TPT

What does it look like to fight with faith? Maybe it
means you stand behind God, letting Him lead the
charge. Maybe it requires you to engage only when
you feel the Lord's leading. Or maybe it means you
take the next right step and trust God to give you
tools for the battle. Regardless, let the takeaway be
that in every conflict your faith has a role to play.

Today, ask God for clarity. Let Him settle your
spirit. Ask how to fight with faith in each circumstance you are facing. Ask God to reveal when
He is battling on your behalf and when you are to
engage. And ask for a new level of bravery so you
can fight with confidence.

*Dear God, help me know how to fight
with faith. I'm not sure what it looks
like and how to make it happen. Please
teach me. In Jesus' name I pray. Amen.*

YOUR FAITH IS STRONG!

Then Jesus answered her, "Dear woman, your faith is strong! What you desire will be done for you." And at that very moment, her daughter was instantly set free from demonic torment.
MATTHEW 15:28 TPT

Don't miss an important truth. The reason the daughter of the woman in this passage was freed from demonic possession was a direct result of the woman's faith. It was her steadfast trust in Jesus—her knowing He could do the miraculous—that ushered in healing. Her belief so delighted Jesus' heart that His response was instant freedom for the girl.

Don't miss the opportunity to ask God for healing. Go to Him in prayer with unwavering faith that what you ask will be done. Be bold in your requests always laced with thanksgiving. And choose to believe that God is who He says He is and that He will do what He says He will do in His Word. Let the Lord say to you, "Dear woman, your faith is strong!"

Dear God, I want my faith to be strong and unshakable. Let me come to You in prayer with courage and confidence in Your goodness. In Jesus' name I pray. Amen.

ENCOURAGING OTHERS

So now, I instruct you before the God of resurrection life and before Jesus, the Anointed One, who demonstrated a beautiful testimony even before Pontius Pilate, that you follow this commission faithfully with a clear conscience and without blemish until the appearing of our Lord Jesus Christ.
1 TIMOTHY 6:13–14 TPT

In this passage of scripture, Paul was encouraging Timothy on the deepest level to walk out the call on his life. He was giving the commission weight by bringing the names of God and Jesus into the conversation. Paul was trying to strengthen his young protégé for the task at hand.

Be the kind of woman who reaches back to help those who need their confidence bolstered. Let your courage be contagious for others. Sometimes we need someone to speak directly into our lives, reminding us that through our faith we are able. Be that person for those around you.

Dear God, open my eyes to see those who need encouragement and hope. Let my words be part of what strengthens their resolve to follow Your will for their lives. In Jesus' name I pray. Amen.

YOUR HUMAN LIMITATIONS

Jesus responded, "What appears humanly impossible is more than possible with God. For God can do what man cannot."

LUKE 18:27 TPT

Be encouraged that success is not always up to you. As a matter of fact, find relief in knowing there are some things that are doable only with God's intervention. So often we beat ourselves up when we fail. We feel bad because our best isn't good enough. And we end up on a performance treadmill, exhausted and striving to do what is humanly impossible.

Take every failure and frustration to God in prayer. Tell Him about the places you feel terribly imperfect. Be honest about where you feel you're falling short. God understands your limitations because He created you. He knows every shortcoming and weakness and deficiency. But from the beginning, His plan has been to fill in those gaps and make up the difference. Ask Him to do that for you.

Dear God, I don't like feeling weak, but it makes me understand my desperate need for You! There are things that require Your help. Give me the courage to ask for it and the confidence to try again. In Jesus' name I pray. Amen.

THE HOLY SPIRIT WITHIN YOU

"Believe in me so that rivers of living water will burst out from within you, flowing from your innermost being, just like the Scripture says!" Jesus was prophesying about the Holy Spirit that believers were being prepared to receive. But the Holy Spirit had not yet been poured out upon them, because Jesus had not yet been unveiled in his full splendor.

JOHN 7:38–39 TPT

Don't forget that the Holy Spirit is with you all the time. When you become a believer, God deposits His Spirit inside you. That means God's presence is with you always. The Spirit is what enables you to walk out a righteous life. He is the prompting you receive—the gut feeling that makes you second-guess a decision. He is the conviction you feel to turn from sinful choices.

If you are a believer, embrace the Holy Spirit. Let His guidance burst out from within you. Let Him make your faith courageous as you follow God's leading in all you do.

Dear God, thank You for the gift of the Holy Spirit. Help me boldly respond to His guidance with faith. In Jesus' name I pray. Amen.

COMPASSION OVER CONDEMNATION

*So stop being critical and condemning of
other believers, but instead determine to
never deliberately cause a brother or sister
to stumble and fall because of your actions.*
ROMANS 14:13 TPT

It's easy to criticize someone else, especially when
their shortcomings are public. It's easy to point
fingers at those who fall short of the standard or
to sit in judgment as someone's shoddy choices
catch up with them. And it takes no effort to think
less of one who has experienced a moral failure.

But it takes courage to stop being critical and
condemning. It takes a bold resolve not to gloat
when others fall. And it takes determination and
compassion to pick others up rather than cause
them to stumble. Ask the Lord to plant deep in your
heart a love for those around you. And be quick to
remove any thoughts that lead you down the path
of anger or resentment.

*Dear God, I want to be known as a woman
who loves others well so Your name is
glorified. Help me develop a kindheartedness
deep inside that can't be undone by time
or trouble. In Jesus' name I pray. Amen.*

GOD KEEPS HIS PROMISES

In spite of all this, his faith in God's promise did not falter. In fact, his faith grew as he gave glory to God because he was supremely confident that God could deliver on His promise. This is why, you see, God saw his faith and counted him as righteous; this is how he became right with God.
ROMANS 4:20–22 VOICE

God's promise was for Abraham and Sarah to have a child. In the natural, this promise seemed impossible. These two were well into their golden years and past childbearing age. But in God's economy, a promise made is a promise kept, and Abraham clung to this truth with courageous faith. As a result, God counted him as righteous.

With God everything is possible. That means He can keep every promise to repair relationships, heal ailments, restore finances, open doors, and perform miracles. Ask God for the courageous faith to believe it.

Dear God, I am in awe of Abraham's faith. Regardless of what it looked like in the natural, his faith never wavered. Help me always to believe that You are working for my benefit and Your glory. In Jesus' name I pray. Amen.

YOUR MEETING PLACE

*The Eternal is my shepherd, He cares for me
always. He provides me rest in rich, green
fields beside streams of refreshing water. He
soothes my fears; He makes me whole again,
steering me off worn, hard paths to roads
where truth and righteousness echo His name.*
PSALM 23:1–3 VOICE

Many of us crave this kind of care for our own lives.
As women, we are so busy caring for everybody
else that we often forget to care about ourselves.
We're focused on making others comfortable and
fulfilling their requests for help. We are always one
step ahead, predicting what those we love may
need next. And so the thought of someone caring
for us feels indulgent.

Let today's scripture passage wash over you
in a fresh way. Visualize the green fields and the
refreshing water. Thank God for providing rest as
He calms your fears. When you need it, let this
be the place you come back to, to meet with God.
And have confident faith that He will be there
every time.

*Dear God, I love having a special place
where I can sit in Your presence and be
restored. In Jesus' name I pray. Amen.*

THE DARK VALLEYS

*Even in the unending shadows of death's darkness,
I am not overcome by fear. Because You are
with me in those dark moments, near with Your
protection and guidance, I am comforted.*
PSALM 23:4 VOICE

God's presence will make you courageous. No matter what's happening in your life, He is the One who will give you the boldness to take the next step. Because the Lord is with you, you'll be able to choose a faith response over one of fear. And even more, you will be comforted through it.

Maybe you're in a dark valley right now. Maybe you're afraid because of circumstances surrounding you. Maybe it feels unending, like there's no way out. Cry to God right now and ask for His hand to grab on to. Let Him be your protector. Let Him be the One who comforts. And let God give you courage to follow Him into the light.

Dear God, help me overcome my fear of these dark moments. Remind me of Your presence. And deliver me from this fear, giving me courageous faith for what's ahead. In Jesus' name I pray. Amen.

A TABLE IN YOUR HONOR

*You spread out a table before me, provisions
in the midst of attack from my enemies;
You care for all my needs, anointing my
head with soothing, fragrant oil, filling my
cup again and again with Your grace.*

PSALM 23:5 VOICE

You may be intimidated by your enemies, but God is not. As a matter of fact, He promises to fill a banquet table in your honor to disrupt their plans. And with God on your side, who could ever win against you?

When your faith is unshakable, you understand this verse on a cellular level. You've watched God meet your needs. You've seen His anointing and favor on your life. You've seen Him restore the broken and lost places in your heart. And you have witnessed the refreshment that gets you back on the battlefield. Once again, take heart in the King as you feast in confidence, regardless of the chaos around you.

Dear God, today's verse is such a beautiful visual of Your awesomeness. Let me find peace in the middle of my mess. Give me a boldness as I trust and wait for You. In Jesus' name I pray. Amen.

ALWAYS AND EVERYWHERE

*Certainly Your faithful protection and
loving provision will pursue me where I
go, always, everywhere. I will always be
with the Eternal, in Your house forever.*
PSALM 23:6 VOICE

Spend time today thanking God for His unmatched love and protection. He has been with you wherever you've gone and will continue to be with you always. There is no place you can go that His love and protection won't be in force. And knowing that God's presence is part of your every moment, let it give you courageous faith to step out and speak up.

Even more, let God's presence be motivation to deepen your relationship with Him. Recognize that He understands the complexity of the emotions you're feeling. He understands the details of your circumstances. And in His sovereignty, God has already provided for every need you will face. Never underestimate the goodness of God as your loving Father! You can have full confidence in His love.

*Dear God, there is great comfort in knowing
You are with me always. And I'm grateful You
offer protection and provision for my life.
Help me embrace all You offer to those who
love You. In Jesus' name I pray. Amen.*

THROUGH YOU

Now to the God who can do so many
awe-inspiring things, immeasurable things,
things greater than we ever could ask or imagine
through the power at work in us, to Him be all glory
in the church and in Jesus the Anointed from this
generation to the next, forever and ever. Amen.
EPHESIANS 3:20–21 VOICE

Have bold faith in our God, who is greater than we could ever imagine. He is uncontainable and undefinable. And in our humanity, we gravely limit His abilities because our minds can only think just so deep. But when we meditate on scripture like today's passage, we gain a greater appreciation for God's magnificence.

You can have courageous faith in a God who can do immeasurable things. You can have confident faith in the One who can do awe-inspiring things. But to understand that He can do these through us is one of the most beautiful blessings available to the believer. That's why God deserves all the glory all the time.

Dear God, use me. Let my life reflect Your
will. Make me fearless to be used to further
Your kingdom. In Jesus' name I pray. Amen.

EVERY STEP OF THE WAY

*No test or temptation that comes your way
is beyond the course of what others have
had to face. All you need to remember is that
God will never let you down; he'll never let
you be pushed past your limit; he'll always
be there to help you come through it.*

1 CORINTHIANS 10:13 MSG

What a relief! Not only will God never let you be pushed past your ability to handle difficulties, but He will be with you every step of the way. God promises to help you come through it, and He will never let you down. He's incapable of it.

So you can be confident that whatever frustrations and fears come your way, whatever temptation or trials present themselves, whatever worry may weigh you down, you are not alone. Just as countless others before you discovered, life doesn't play fair. But with God on your side, you will find victory.

*Dear God, thank You for promising to be
with me every step of the way. Thank You
for knowing my limitations and for Your
promise to honor them. You are a good,
good Father. In Jesus' name I pray. Amen.*

LOVE'S MEASUREMENTS

*I ask that he will strengthen you in your inner selves
from the riches of his glory through the Spirit.
I ask that Christ will live in your hearts through
faith. As a result of having strong roots in love,
I ask that you'll have the power to grasp love's
width and length, height and depth, together
with all believers. I ask that you'll know the love
of Christ that is beyond knowledge so that you
will be filled entirely with the fullness of God.*
EPHESIANS 3:16–19 CEB

Paul prayed this powerful prayer for the Ephesians.
His hope was for them to have roots firmly secured
in God's love. And it was because of those roots
that Paul was asking God for a fresh revelation. He
wanted the Ephesians to understand the immea-
surability of God's love for them.

It takes courage to embrace God's love because
we simply can't fathom the width and length and
height and depth of it. Faith means we choose to
believe anyway.

*Dear God, thank You for loving me
immeasurably. Let that encourage my
heart today. In Jesus' name I pray. Amen.*

THE HARVEST OF YOUR FAITH

*You love him passionately although you have
not seen him, but through believing in him you
are saturated with an ecstatic joy, indescribably
sublime and immersed in glory. For you are
reaping the harvest of your faith—the full
salvation promised you—your souls' victory!*
1 PETER 1:8–9 TPT

Have you ever considered that there is a harvest of
your faith? Some might call these blessings. Others
might refer to them as God hugs or God winks. Still
others might describe the harvest as times when
God showed up. Regardless, your unrelenting faith
brings beautiful things your way.

Choose to be all in! Don't waver in your faith.
Don't wait until you clean up your act before you
become a believer. Don't be lukewarm. Instead, love
God passionately, trusting He is woven throughout
your life even though you can't see Him with your
eyes. Boldly believe and reap the harvest.

*Dear God, help me keep my eyes focused on
You in every circumstance. Let me see You
moving throughout my life in meaningful ways.
And grow my faith so that I will receive the
blessings from it. In Jesus' name I pray. Amen.*

BE READY TO SHARE

But exalt Him as Lord in your heart. Always be
ready to offer a defense, humbly and respectfully,
when someone asks why you live in hope. Keep
your conscience clear so that those who ridicule
your good conduct in the Anointed and say
bad things about you will be put to shame.
1 PETER 3:15–16 VOICE

Be ready to share your testimony with others. In humility and honor, courageously unpack your story of faith when God makes a way. This world needs hope. This world needs to know there's something better—something different. And God is the answer.

Ask the Lord to bring clarity to your mind so you can present your thoughts in powerful ways. Ask for the words to share with others. Ask Him for passion that others can see. And be respectful as you pass on the magnificent and breathtaking moments when God's mighty hand moved in your life.

Dear God, I am excited for opportunities
where I can share hope with the world.
Use my testimony to bring glory to Your
name. What a privilege and honor to boast
about You! In Jesus' name I pray. Amen.

SHAPING YOUR LIFE

*As God's obedient children, never again shape
your lives by the desires that you followed when
you didn't know better. Instead, shape your lives
to become like the Holy One who called you.*
1 PETER 1:14–15 TPT

Simply put, now that you know what sinful living looks like, choose to follow the path of righteous living. Before you became a believer, you didn't understand the difference between *your* way and the *world's* way. Chances are you had a skewed view of right and wrong and didn't understand the penalties and consequences that came with sinful choices. But then you accepted the gift of salvation.

Let God give you courage to shape your life in ways that glorify His name. Ask for discernment and wisdom every day. Listen to the Holy Spirit, who will lead you in the right ways. And turn from the sinful nature that has woven its way through your life, letting God untangle your heart as you pursue living right with Him.

*Dear God, give me courage to turn away from
my old sins, letting every word and action
point to You. In Jesus' name I pray. Amen.*

REPAYING BAD WITH A BLESSING

Finally, all of you, be like-minded and show sympathy, love, compassion, and humility to and for each other—not paying back evil with evil or insult with insult, but repaying the bad with a blessing. It was this you were called to do, so that you might inherit a blessing.

1 PETER 3:8–9 VOICE

Repaying evil with a blessing takes confidence and courage. So often when our feelings get hurt we lash out. Being kind in response is not our default, because that's not where our heart is in the moment. But God is asking us to do better in how we treat others because it matters to Him.

Responding with kindness when someone is snarky takes God's help. Being compassionate to the catty also requires God's grace. And answering the hurtful with humility takes faith. Ask God to soften your heart, enabling you to repay bad with a blessing, knowing you'll be blessed in return.

Dear God, I need Your help. Make me fearless and fruitful as I try to live with compassion and love, even to those who hurt me. In Jesus' name I pray. Amen.

FULL OF LOVE FOR OTHERS

Now, because of your obedience to the truth,
you have purified your very souls, and this
empowers you to be full of love for your fellow
believers. So express this sincere love toward one
another passionately and with a pure heart.
1 PETER 1:22 TPT

Today's verse offers a powerful challenge to love others boldly. It's a call to be sincere and passionate, with a pure heart and honest motives. And we are able to do this only because we have anchored our faith in God. Our obedience to what His Word commands matters.

God isn't asking us to love other believers halfheartedly. He won't accept lackluster love either. As a matter of fact, He knows that if we invest time in His presence and choose to follow His ways, our hearts will desire to love others with passion and purpose. When we have courageous faith, we will love courageously.

Dear God, strengthen me in You so that I am able
to be full of love for others. Bless my obedience,
empowering me to show sincere compassion to
friends and family and even to strangers who
cross my path. In Jesus' name I pray. Amen.

THE COURAGE TO
TURN AROUND

*Walk away from the evil things in the world—
just leave them behind, and do what is right,
and always seek peace and pursue it. For the
Lord watches over the righteous, and His ears
are attuned to their prayers. But His face is set
against His enemies; He will punish evildoers.*
1 PETER 3:11–12 VOICE

Just turn around and go the other way when the
Holy Spirit convicts you about the path you're on.
When you hear a whisper warning you of the chaos
ahead or the natural consequences you will face, be
courageous enough to choose differently.

Blessings come to those who do what is right,
pursuing peace and righteous living. Scripture says
God's ears are always listening for the voice of those
who love Him. So be quick to ask for discernment
and wisdom to live your life in a way that glorifies
the Lord. Ask for bravery to stand your ground
when following evil is easier.

*Dear God, I confess the times I've ignored Your
voice and followed my fleshly desires. Help me to be
faithful in all things. In Jesus' name I pray. Amen.*

BEAUTIFUL FRUIT

But the fruit of the Spirit is love, joy, peace, patience, kindness, goodness, faithfulness, gentleness, and self-control. There is no law against things like this. Those who belong to Christ Jesus have crucified the self with its passions and its desires.
GALATIANS 5:22–24 CEB

When you become a believer, beautiful fruit is planted deep inside you that comes into fruition through the Holy Spirit's guidance. Just like fruit starts from seeds in nature and grows through time and care, the fruit in you follows suit. You don't automatically have full access, because it takes life experiences and divine intervention to mature these gifts.

It also requires obedience. For you to exhibit patience, you would have had gritty moments when you learned to wait on God. For you to be gentle and kind, you would have asked Him to help you love unconditionally. Becoming faithful means you've made hard choices to trust when it felt impossible. Yes, maturing fruit involves courage. Ask God to help.

Dear God, I appreciate the fruit of the Spirit and how it blesses others, proves good for me, and glorifies You. Please grow it in me! In Jesus' name I pray. Amen.

FOLLOW YOUR HEART

The heart that believes in him receives the gift of the righteousness of God—and then the mouth confesses, resulting in salvation. For the Scriptures encourage us with these words: "Everyone who believes in him will never be disappointed."
ROMANS 10:10–11 TPT

Salvation starts with the heart, doesn't it? Your belief causes a ripple effect that results in salvation. Once you accept Jesus' invitation to become a child of God by believing that His death on the cross paid your sin debt and washed you clean in the Father's eyes, your eternity in heaven is secured. Scripture says we will not be disappointed with that decision.

Don't waste time trying to earn your salvation by cleaning yourself up or doing good works. Instead, run into His open arms and accept the redemptive work of Jesus. Boldly follow your heart and pray for His presence to steady your faith every day.

Dear God, I believe in You. I believe in the finished work of the cross through Your Son, Jesus. Let me live every day encouraged by this beautiful gift. In Jesus' name I pray. Amen.

WHAT FREEDOM MEANS

You were called to freedom, brothers and sisters; only don't let this freedom be an opportunity to indulge your selfish impulses, but serve each other through love. All the Law has been fulfilled in a single statement: Love your neighbor as yourself.
GALATIANS 5:13–14 CEB

So often we decide that freedom means we can do anything we want to do. We become bold for all the wrong reasons, thinking no one can tell us how to act. And we embrace our selfish desires all in the name of liberty. We're unable to love our neighbors because we're too busy loving ourselves. Even more, the only ones we serve are ourselves.

But it takes a courageous faith to understand the limitations of freedom and honor them. It's not about serving yourself and your impulses. Instead, it's about standing up for what's right and understanding the value of following God's will and ways, choosing to surrender every time.

Dear God, help me not to take advantage of the freedom You offer. Instead, give me a bold desire to serve others in Your name. Give me discernment so I can walk faithfully. In Jesus' name I pray. Amen.

WHERE IS YOUR TREASURE?

*"Don't hoard treasure down here where it
gets eaten by moths and corroded by rust
or—worse!—stolen by burglars. Stockpile
treasure in heaven, where it's safe from moth
and rust and burglars. It's obvious, isn't it? The
place where your treasure is, is the place you
will most want to be, and end up being."*

MATTHEW 6:19–21 MSG

Where do you invest your time and treasure? Today's
passage of scripture is challenging you to decide.
It's easy to collect earthly things. Every day we
invest in earthly relationships and careers and the
latest trends. And while that's not all bad, when it
becomes your sole focus and the desire of your
heart, it is setting you up for heartbreak.

What does it look like to stockpile treasure
in heaven instead? In your opinion, how do you
invest in what pays eternal dividends? Ask God for
insight. Ask for a boldness to choose what can only
be stockpiled in the Lord's house. And let it be a
reflection of your heart.

*Dear God, give me eyes to see life from an
eternal perspective. In Jesus' name I pray. Amen.*

EMBRACING THE NEW

The actions that are produced by selfish motives are obvious, since they include sexual immorality, moral corruption, doing whatever feels good, idolatry, drug use and casting spells, hate, fighting, obsession, losing your temper, competitive opposition, conflict, selfishness, group rivalry, jealousy, drunkenness, partying, and other things like that. I warn you as I have already warned you, that those who do these kinds of things won't inherit God's kingdom.
GALATIANS 5:19–21 CEB

Once you commit your life to Jesus Christ as your Savior and Lord, the Holy Spirit comes to live inside you. He is the One who sounds the alarm bell when you begin to fall into old behavior. Because you're a new creation in Him, because you have been born again, your life is now being shaped and molded so you can be in a right relationship with God. Simply put, a constant transformation is taking place to make you more like Jesus.

Ask God for faith that courageously embraces change and confidently trusts Him through it.

Dear God, thank You for loving me enough to bring about necessary changes for my good and Your glory. In Jesus' name I pray. Amen.

BLESSING OR BOASTING?

"When you demonstrate generosity, do it with
pure motives and without drawing attention
to yourself. Give secretly and your Father,
who sees all you do, will reward you openly."
MATTHEW 6:3–4 TPT

The message we take from Jesus' admonition in this passage is that we shouldn't bless others with the hope of positive and public recognition. We don't need to grandstand. Our endgame shouldn't be bragging rights. Instead, we should give from a place of compassion and humility. Our focus should be to help others rather than to garner praise for ourselves.

This requires God's help. Many times our desire is blessing, but our motivation has a hint of boasting. Before you extend kindness or write a check, go before the throne and ask God to make your heart right. Make sure your reasons for showing generosity are genuine so you can be certain it's not about you.

Dear God, I confess the times I've given with
the hopes of receiving something in return.
Please make my heart clean and my motives
pure so I can boldly be Your hands and feet
without inserting myself. I want all the glory
to be Yours! In Jesus' name I pray. Amen.

THE STING OF REJECTION

Even though He came to His own people,
they refused to listen and receive Him. But
for all who did receive and trust in Him, He
gave them the right to be reborn as children
of God; He bestowed this birthright not by
human power or initiative but by God's will.
JOHN 1:11–13 VOICE

Just like Jesus, there are times we're the ones rejected by our own people. Some family members may not want to know about Jesus and shut us down every time we try to share our faith. The changing dynamics in a relationship when one person becomes a Christian sometimes rocks the boat too much.

How wonderful that we have a Savior who understands our human struggles. He knows what rejection and abandonment feel like, and He understands the complexity of emotions that go with them. Even more, the Lord recognizes the courageous faith it takes to stand strong in what we believe as we face rebuff. Let Him hold you up and renew your strength.

Dear God, give me perspective when I'm
rejected for my faith. Build my confidence
in You alone. In Jesus' name I pray. Amen.

DON'T WORRY

"This is why I tell you to never be worried about your life, for all that you need will be provided, such as food, water, clothing—everything your body needs. Isn't there more to your life than a meal? Isn't your body more than clothing?"
MATTHEW 6:25 TPT

You can be confident that God will provide for your every need every time. Scripture is very clear that we're not to worry about our lives. We aren't to stress about necessities like food and clothing. Because when we obsess about those things, we are doubting God's ability to be God.

Be a courageous believer! Choose to trust the Word to be true, alive, and active. Every promise recorded in the Bible will come to pass because God is unable to contradict Himself. He doesn't change His mind. And everything He does is for your good and His glory. So be bold in your belief and stand firm in your conviction that every need will be met in the right way and at the right time.

Dear God, create in me an unshakable faith that never doubts Your goodness or ability. In Jesus' name I pray. Amen.

HE PLANNED YOUR FUTURE

I know the plans I have in mind for you, declares the LORD; they are plans for peace, not disaster, to give you a future filled with hope.

JEREMIAH 29:11 CEB

If God already knows the plans He created for your life, why is your heart anxious? And if the indisputable Word of God is clear, saying He's made provision for peace and hope to fill your days, why stress? Consider that when you let your heart be troubled, it's a lack of courageous faith. And that kind of living does not glorify God or benefit you.

Choose today to deepen your relationship with your heavenly Father so you can be a bold believer in God's will and ways. Spend time in the Word. Saturate yourself in His presence through prayer. Find like-minded people to do life with. And ask the Lord to fill you with unshakable faith in His unchangeable love.

Dear God, thank You for being involved in the details of my life. Thank You for filling my future with peace and hope. Give me courage to bravely walk it out in faith. In Jesus' name I pray. Amen.

SEEKING GOD'S KINGDOM

"So above all, constantly seek God's kingdom and his righteousness, then all these less important things will be given to you abundantly. Refuse to worry about tomorrow, but deal with each challenge that comes your way, one day at a time. Tomorrow will take care of itself."

MATTHEW 6:33–34 TPT

What a magnificent reminder this passage is to keep our eyes securely focused on the Lord. Every time we look away and stare at our circumstances, it's a setup for discouragement and disappointment. No matter the giants before us, we'll experience courageous faith as we choose to constantly seek God for help. His presence will strengthen us.

Make a commitment to know God better because that intimacy with Him will fuel your fearless faith. He's the One to remove anxiety about tomorrow. God will give you all that's needed for the battle. Seek God's kingdom and His righteousness first and always.

Dear God, I cannot do this without You. Every time I try on my own, I fail and become fearful. Help me seek Your kingdom and Your righteousness every day. In Jesus' name I pray. Amen.

THE INVITATION TO SEARCH

When you call me and come and pray to me, I will listen to you. When you search for me, yes, search for me with all your heart, you will find me.
JEREMIAH 29:12–13 CEB

Be fearless as you search for God. Don't relent in your pursuit of the truth. Scripture makes it clear that you have the opportunity to come into His presence through prayer, asking for what is heavy on your heart. And because He is your gracious Father, He will listen with delight and intensity to everything you say.

The Lord wants to be known by those who love Him, and you are invited to search with passion. So test His Word. Explore scripture for comfort, strength, and wisdom. Through prayer, ask God those deep questions and share the puzzling thoughts about who He is and what He has said He will do. God promises to be found by those who seek in earnest.

Dear God, I want to know You better. I want a deeper understanding of Your goodness and sovereignty. Open my eyes and give me clarity. In Jesus' name I pray. Amen.

A LAST HOPE

Just then a woman who had hemorrhaged for twelve years slipped in from behind and lightly touched his robe. She was thinking to herself, "If I can just put a finger on his robe, I'll get well." Jesus turned—caught her at it. Then he reassured her: "Courage, daughter. You took a risk of faith, and now you're well." The woman was well from then on.
MATTHEW 9:20–22 MSG

Of all the amazing stories in the Bible, this woman's points directly to courageous faith. Her condition had left her physically weak, socially unclean, and financially broke, and she was out of hope. She had exhausted every option imaginable up to this point, but then she heard about Jesus.

Think of the courage it took to leave her home to seek Him out. Think of the faith it took to believe that just touching His garment would heal her of a twelve-year ailment. And think of the praise and gratitude that resulted from her healing.

Dear God, remind me that when I am out of hope and desperate for change, You are always within reach. In Jesus' name I pray. Amen.

A LITTLE WHILE LONGER

*So don't throw away your confidence—it brings
a great reward. You need to endure so that you
can receive the promises after you do God's will.
In a little while longer, the one who is coming
will come and won't delay; but my righteous
one will live by faith, and my whole being won't
be pleased with anyone who shrinks back.*
HEBREWS 10:35–38 CEB

Keep on keepin' on! We are being encouraged to
stay the course because our endurance will be
rewarded. Think about how often we want to give
up and throw in the towel when things get hard. We
want to quit because the battle is overwhelming.
We're emotionally exhausted. But every time we
stay in the game and activate our courageous faith
in God, it will be for our good and His glory.

Ask the Lord to make you brave. Ask Him to
increase your perseverance in the hard seasons
as you draw strength from Him to stay engaged a
little while longer.

*Dear God, give me the confidence necessary to
stay focused on You as I navigate the struggles
that come my way. In Jesus' name I pray. Amen.*

BEING CALLED UP

Since My servant Moses is now dead, you and the Israelites must prepare to cross over the Jordan River to enter the land I have given you. I will give you every place you walk, wherever your feet touch, just as I promised Moses.

JOSHUA 1:2–3 VOICE

Imagine finding out you're no longer the runner-up, but the main person! The truth is it's often so much easier to watch others lead than do it ourselves. The risks are less. The consequences are fewer. And we don't have to worry about getting it wrong, because the responsibility doesn't rest on our shoulders.

But we can take heart because God is present! And while we must initiate the steps forward in faith, He will guide them. He will prepare the path ahead. He will build our confidence. And even more, God will bless the obedience it takes to follow Him courageously when we're being called up.

Dear God, help me to be brave when You ask me to step out of my comfort zone and into Your will for my life. I need Your encouragement. In Jesus' name I pray. Amen.

OFFERING YOUR LIFE TO GOD

For the Lord our God has brought us his glory-light. I offer him my life in joyous sacrifice. Tied tightly to your altar, I will bring you praise. For you are the God of my life and I lift you high, exalting you to the highest place. So let's keep on giving our thanks to God, for he is so good! His constant, tender love lasts forever!
PSALM 118:27–29 TPT

What does offering your life to God mean to you? To the psalmist it meant sacrificing his will for God's will—and doing so with joy. It meant living to glorify God with his life—both in words and actions. And it involved an intentionality to bring the Lord praise through sacrificial living.

Putting God's will above your desires takes grit. Making Him the Lord of your life takes brave choices every day. But the beautiful result is being lavished in His love for all of eternity. What a big blessing for a small sacrifice.

Dear God, in humility and honor, I offer You my life. Lead me in Your ways. In Jesus' name I pray. Amen.

ROOTED IN THE WORD

Let the words from the book of the law be always
on your lips. Meditate on them day and night so
that you may be careful to live by all that is written
in it. If you do, as you make your way through this
world, you will prosper and always find success.
JOSHUA 1:8 VOICE

If you want courageous faith, let the Word of God be your guide every day. Cling to the scriptures that speak directly to your situation. Memorize them. Write them on note cards. Tape them to your mirror. And every time you begin to feel weak, fearful, or discouraged, go right back to the verses that encourage your heart.

God's Word is power packed with truth, helping you navigate life. Need wisdom or strength or a heavenly perspective? Need confirmation or help with difficult decisions? Dig into scripture. The only way to live with a victory mindset is to have your faith deeply rooted in the Bible.

Dear God, thank You for revealing Yourself
through Your Word. Let it be the resource I reach
for every day! In Jesus' name I pray. Amen.

GOD'S PROVISION

I am convinced that my God will fully satisfy every need you have, for I have seen the abundant riches of glory revealed to me through Jesus Christ! And God our Father will receive all the glory and the honor throughout the eternity of eternities! Amen!
PHILIPPIANS 4:19–20 TPT

Imagine living with that kind of confidence! What if you wholeheartedly believed that every one of your needs would be met? Instead of freaking out about finances, what if you trusted God for provision? When you needed wisdom, what if you waited with expectation for God's revelation? When battling loneliness, what if you believed God was preparing community for you? Choosing this mindset is courageous faith.

Let God know where you need His glory to shine. Talk to Him about the desert places in your life. Ask the Lord to remind you of times when He has blessed you before. And ask for the courage to believe and trust in His immeasurable love, knowing His provision flows from it.

Dear God, forgive me for doubting Your goodness. You're kind and generous, lavishing love freely. I believe that no matter where I am lacking, You will meet every need every time. In Jesus' name I pray. Amen.

117

THE POWER OF HIS PRESENCE

This is My command: be strong and courageous.
Never be afraid or discouraged because I
am your God, the Eternal One, and I will
remain with you wherever you go.
JOSHUA 1:9 VOICE

Because of God's continual presence in your life, you can be brave. And because of His holiness, you can maintain a positive outlook on life. You may not always understand God's ways, but by faith you can trust that He is always with you wherever you go.

There are so many things to be afraid of in today's world. We fear more than we realize. From broken relationships to financial ruin to a decline in health, circumstances sometimes cause us to want to climb into bed and pull the covers over our heads. But as a believer, you can choose faith instead. Ask the Lord to make you aware of His presence so you will be comforted and strengthened.

Dear God, I realize I can only experience
true strength and courage when it comes
from Your continual presence in my life.
Help me remember to lean on You above
all else. In Jesus' name I pray. Amen.

DIVINE TRANSFER

Our faith in Jesus transfers God's righteousness
to us and he now declares us flawless in his eyes.
This means we can now enjoy true and lasting
peace with God, all because of what our Lord
Jesus, the Anointed One, has done for us.
ROMANS 5:1 TPT

Imagine being seen as flawless. In a world full of imperfection, what an unexpected gift to know we're declared unblemished in God's eyes. Regardless of our bad choices and seasons of sinning, once we commit our lives to Jesus as our Savior and Lord, a divine transfer takes place. And supernaturally, we are made right with God. We are seen as spotless.

Thank Him as you pray, recognizing the blessing of redemption. Let this beautiful gift create a deeper appreciation for the Father's love. Let it secure your belief, making it unshakable. And praise God for seeing you through the blood of Jesus rather than the shame of sin.

Dear God, it's a privilege to be made clean by
the blood of Jesus, and I am in awe of how You
think of everything. I am grateful for the gift
of eternity. In Jesus' name I pray. Amen.

WHO CAN YOU TRUST?

*Lord, it is so much better to trust in you to save
me than to put my confidence in someone else.
Yes, it is so much better to trust in the Lord to
save me than to put my confidence in celebrities.*
PSALM 118:8–9 TPT

Be careful not to place your complete trust in anyone but God. Even those who have pure motives
and great intentions can let you down. You'll experience betrayal from those you consider reliable
and dependable. And no doubt you'll become tired
of the heartbreak that comes from being deceived.

The only hope is to anchor your confidence in
the Lord alone. Through prayer and petition, He
will teach you to manage expectations with family
and friends and others who make big promises.
And with each passing day, you will find strength
and encouragement through your relationship with
God. He will prove Himself trustworthy.

*Dear God, keep my heart from becoming hardened
by disappointment in others. Instead, let my heart
be full of gratitude for all the ways You have kept
Your word to me. In Jesus' name I pray. Amen.*

HE IS USING EVERYTHING

*But that's not all! Even in times of trouble we
have a joyful confidence, knowing that our
pressures will develop in us patient endurance.
And patient endurance will refine our character,
and proven character leads us back to hope.*
ROMANS 5:3–4 TPT

When you hold on to courageous faith in times of
trouble, you can trust that God will reward your
choice. The Bible tells us that He wastes nothing. So
even when your life is a mess, He is maturing things
in you. He is using your circumstances to grow you
and change you. It's a supernatural process.

But we must be willing to stay present and lean
on God for help. We have to decide that there's
value in activating our faith boldly. And even more,
we must praise God through the storm, knowing
that He is using everything for our good and His
glory. Because of God's faithfulness to the process,
we can have joy, confidence, endurance, hope, and
a proven character.

*Dear God, I don't just want to hold on in hard
times. I want to thrive through them, confident
that You're growing me into the woman You
intended. In Jesus' name I pray. Amen.*

PRAYING FOR OTHERS

We always thank God for all of you when we mention you constantly in our prayers. This is because we remember your work that comes from faith, your effort that comes from love, and your perseverance that comes from hope in our Lord Jesus Christ in the presence of our God and Father.

1 THESSALONIANS 1:2–3 CEB

Committing to pray for others is a powerful promise with eternal benefits. If you offer to do so, be sure to follow through. Ask God to help them navigate their situation. Ask Him for healing. Ask the Lord to provide strength and wisdom. Ask for peace and comfort in difficult times. But be bold as you take them to the throne room.

Pray because you know it works. Pray because those you are praying for believe in its power. Pray because you know God answers at the right time and in the right ways. And pray because you committed to it. Every time they come to mind, lift their names up to the Father.

Dear God, it is a privilege to pray for others. Help me to be a committed prayer warrior for those I love. In Jesus' name I pray. Amen.

NO DISCRIMINATION

Now, would anyone dare to die for the sake of a wicked person? We can all understand if someone was willing to die for a truly noble person. But Christ proved God's passionate love for us by dying in our place while we were still lost and ungodly!
ROMANS 5:7–8 TPT

What a bold decision by God. He didn't take the easy route, choosing to love only the lovable. He didn't cherry-pick who would receive His blessing based on their standing or their actions. Instead, God sent His Son to die for everyone. Jesus' blood covers both the humble and loyal as well as the wretched and despicable. It was spilled for the miserable and heartbroken and for those who feel worthless and inferior.

Let this passage strengthen your gratitude for Jesus' gift of salvation. Let it lead you toward courageous faith, knowing nothing can disqualify you from God's love. Even more, share this good news with others so they understand that the Lord doesn't discriminate. This beautiful blessing is for all and leads to eternity in heaven.

Dear God, thank You that the blood of Jesus is all-inclusive. In His name I pray. Amen.

THE COURAGE TO BE CONTENT WITH YOURSELF

So be content with who you are, and don't put on airs. God's strong hand is on you; he'll promote you at the right time. Live carefree before God; he is most careful with you.
1 PETER 5:6–7 MSG

Being content with yourself takes courage. We often think the grass is greener on the other side. We may be smart but wish we were beautiful. We may be kind but wish we were witty. We may be fantastic at parenting but wish we were a better cook. And in our insecurity, so often we act like we have it all together and lack for nothing.

Allow today's scripture to build your faith. It's vital to understand that God knows what He's doing with your life. His timing is perfect and His will will be done. Once you accept this as truth, you'll find grace to be happy—happy in who God created you to be. And that will breed contentment and confidence.

Dear God, help me trust in who You made me to be rather than second-guess myself. In Jesus' name I pray. Amen.

PROMISES ATTACHED TO FAITH

But those who trust in the Eternal One will regain their strength. They will soar on wings as eagles. They will run—never winded, never weary. They will walk—never tired, never faint.

ISAIAH 40:31 VOICE

How do you usually handle difficult moments? Do you retreat in defeat? Do you hide under a blanket, hoping everything will fix itself? Maybe you become angry and annoyed. Or do you take your frustration out on those around you? Today's scripture tells us that when we feel overwhelmed and ineffective, trusting in God is key. He is the One who will make our faith courageous again. The Lord will give us divine endurance to stay present.

The next time you're tempted to respond to life's hardships in unhealthy ways, reach out to God in prayer. Take a step back before reacting in haste and talk to your Father in heaven. There are beautiful promises attached to faith, and they are yours for the taking.

Dear God, help me trust in You over everything else. All I need I can get from You, and I am humbled. In Jesus' name I pray. Amen.

SUFFERING HAS AN END DATE

So keep a firm grip on the faith. The suffering won't last forever. It won't be long before this generous God who has great plans for us in Christ—eternal and glorious plans they are!— will have you put together and on your feet for good. He gets the last word; yes, he does.
1 PETER 5:10–11 MSG

When scripture says the suffering we're experiencing "won't last forever," let it soothe your weary heart. It's a promise to sink your teeth into because it gives hope for much-needed relief. We have limits to the pain our heart can handle. So knowing that this season of suffering has an end date allows us to exhale in gratitude to the Lord.

Ask God to give you courage to stand strong in your faith. Ask for perspective, knowing that His plans are eternal and glorious. Let Him strengthen you, setting your feet on solid ground. And don't ever forget that God is good and He is sovereign. Suffering doesn't have to be a destabilizer if you have a firm grip on faith.

Dear God, be with me in the suffering.
In Jesus' name I pray. Amen.

NEVER FADES OR WITHERS

The grass withers, the flower fades as the breath of the Eternal One blows away. People are no different from grass. The grass withers, the flower fades; nothing lasts except the word of our God. It will stand forever.

Isaiah 40:7–8 voice

What a blessing to know that God's Word isn't subject to the effects of aging. It never grows old, and it never loses power. The promises written on its pages don't expire, nor does it become irrelevant. The Bible is alive and active in your life right now, whether you recognize it or not. So don't forgo digging deep into scripture for hope and perspective; know that God will meet you there every time.

In this world, we are conditioned to know things wither over time. We understand there's a shelf life and an expiration date. In real time, we watch our own bodies weaken and deteriorate. But God is the same today as yesterday and tomorrow. So is His Word. Let that encourage you today.

Dear God, I'm so grateful that You are untouched by the effects of time. It blesses me to know You're unchangeable! In Jesus' name I pray. Amen.

KEEP WATCH AND STAY ALERT

Keep a cool head. Stay alert. The Devil is poised to pounce, and would like nothing better than to catch you napping. Keep your guard up. You're not the only ones plunged into these hard times. It's the same with Christians all over the world.
1 PETER 5:8–9 MSG

Why is it important to have courageous faith? Today's scripture answers that question with certainty. Because we have an enemy who wants to discourage and destroy, we have to not only trust God but trust Him courageously! We must trust Him without question, wielding a bold belief that since God is for us, no weapon forged against us can prosper.

So we live with our eyes wide open and focused on the goodness of God. We stay alert, being aware of when negative thoughts or feelings try to land. Our guard is always up as we take inventory of our heart. And we remember we're not alone because believers all over the world struggle with the same enemy. Together we are strong.

Dear God, make me courageous as I stand strong against the enemy's schemes for my life. In Jesus' name I pray. Amen.

WEAVING TOGETHER

So we are convinced that every detail of our lives is continually woven together for good, for we are his lovers who have been called to fulfill his designed purpose.
ROMANS 8:28 TPT

We can have confident faith knowing that God works everything in our lives for His glory and our good. Somehow, in His sovereignty, the Lord weaves together every situation we encounter. He supernaturally fits pieces together seamlessly. God understands the complexity of timing for each moment so we experience maximum benefits. And He wastes nothing because He sees the value in everything.

Saying you trust God isn't a careless comment or an honest hope. Instead, let it be a battle cry to encourage your heart to hold on. Let it be what drives you to surrender your fear again. And when everything feels chaotic and messy, know that God doesn't see it that way. He is untangling each strand and weaving something beautiful.

Dear God, help me believe that You are in the middle of my messy circumstances. Let me cling with all my might to faith, believing I will see Your goodness in action. In Jesus' name I pray. Amen.

THE DEAL WITH FEAR

*Be strong and brave, and don't tremble in fear
of them, because the Eternal your God is going
with you. He'll never fail you or abandon you!*
DEUTERONOMY 31:6 VOICE

Fear is a big deal. As a matter of fact, God addresses that topic over 360 times in the Bible. He knew fear would be something we would struggle with from time to time. And God's constant reminder is to be strong and brave *because* He is with us. Our heavenly Father knows us so well, understanding being brave on our own is futile.

The next time fear creeps in, remember that God is with you in that very moment. He is closer than your next breath. So talk to Him right then and there about the fear you're feeling. Let Him know what's causing your anxious heart to beat out of your chest. Tell Him your worries. And ask God to give you a fearlessness secured by His presence. Ask for courageous faith.

*Dear God, You know my battle with fear. Please
make me brave, especially knowing You promise
to be with me always. In Jesus' name I pray. Amen.*

INCOMPARABLE

I am convinced that any suffering we endure is less than nothing compared to the magnitude of glory that is about to be unveiled within us. The entire universe is standing on tiptoe, yearning to see the unveiling of God's glorious sons and daughters!
ROMANS 8:18–19 TPT

We can't compare our current suffering with the glory we will experience when we meet the Father. We will deal with hard things in this life. We will face joy-draining and spine-weakening moments when we feel we can't go on. Our foundation will be shaken. To think anything different will set us up for heartache. But we must keep an eternal perspective.

Our minds can't imagine the awesomeness of what's coming. We are mentally unable to grasp the display of the goodness God has prepared for His sons and daughters. So until that day happens, be brave and trust the Lord. This life is a breath, and God has fully equipped us to navigate it.

Dear God, give me divine perspective so I don't lose sight of the glory to come. In Jesus' name I pray. Amen.

GENERATIONAL BLESSINGS

*That precious memory triggers another:
your honest faith—and what a rich faith it is,
handed down from your grandmother Lois
to your mother Eunice, and now to you! And
the special gift of ministry you received when
I laid hands on you and prayed—keep that
ablaze! God doesn't want us to be shy with
his gifts, but bold and loving and sensible.*

2 TIMOTHY 1:5–7 MSG

When you are bold with your faith, sharing God's
hand in your life with your family, you create a gen-
erational blessing. So often the best way to share
your testimony is to live it in real time. Words can
be cheap, but actions speak volumes.

Don't forget that your children and grand-
children are watching how you navigate life. They
notice the way you handle anger. They see who
gets the glory. They recognize when you're fully
trusting the Lord and when you are leaning on your
own strength. Ask God to help you live a bold and
honest faith that points to Him.

*Dear God, I know the goal isn't perfection
but purposeful living. Help my life influence
others for You. In Jesus' name I pray. Amen.*

WHERE DOES YOUR MOTIVATION COME FROM?

*Those who are motivated by the flesh only pursue
what benefits themselves. But those who live by
the impulses of the Holy Spirit are motivated
to pursue spiritual realities. For the sense and
reason of the flesh is death, but the mind-set
controlled by the Spirit finds life and peace.*
ROMANS 8:5–6 TPT

Once you become a believer, God's plan is for
you to live by the Holy Spirit's promptings. You
must make the choice to set aside what your flesh
wants and the ways you used to do things. You must
decide to set aside your selfish desires. You can't
go to the empty well of the world and expect a
satisfying drink.

Ask the Father to renew your mind through
His Spirit. Ask for spiritual eyes and ears to see
His plan for your life. Let God embolden you to
embrace faith, letting Him be your driving force
and your true north.

*Dear God, let my motivation come from You
and not from anything the world strategically
offers. Help me set aside my own desires and
seek Yours. In Jesus' name I pray. Amen.*

STAY WITH GOD

*I'm sure now I'll see God's goodness in the
exuberant earth. Stay with GOD! Take heart.
Don't quit. I'll say it again: Stay with GOD.*
PSALM 27:13–14 MSG

When faced with trials and trauma, we usually
choose one of two responses: We either run to
God or run in the other direction. We cry out to Him
in desperation or sob alone in our pillow. Quitting
is the easy way out of a heartbreaking situation.
But it takes real courage to stay with God when
everything looks like a dead end.

Scripture tells us we can do all things through
Christ who strengthens us. Giving up never has to
be an option when we secure our faith in the Father.
Let Him give you strength and perseverance and
motivation to keep going. Every time you involve
the Lord in the circumstances of your life, beautiful
things emerge.

*Dear God, make me a brave woman of faith.
I'm tired of placing my hope in the wrong
things or hiding when life gets hard. Help me
stay with You, knowing You'll guide me through
to victory. In Jesus' name I pray. Amen.*

ACCEPTED BY GOD

*And you did not receive the "spirit of religious
duty," leading you back into the fear of never being
good enough. But you have received the "Spirit
of full acceptance," enfolding you into the family
of God. And you will never feel orphaned, for as
he rises up within us, our spirits join him in saying
the words of tender affection, "Beloved Father!"*
ROMANS 8:15 TPT

When we feel like our performance is part of our
faith, we will always fall short. Trying to be good
enough for God will be our undoing because we
will drown in shame. While we may be on the performance treadmill in life, our faith experience is
drenched in grace. Jesus' blood covers every failure
and shortcoming.

You're fully accepted by God not because of
anything you've done. You could never earn your
salvation, which is why God made a way for you
through His Son. Don't complicate the blessing.
Be confident in the Lord's approval.

*Dear God, thank You for not making me earn
my way into heaven. Jesus' blood is enough,
and I know it. In His name I pray. Amen.*

WHEN A PARENT LEAVES

You've always been right there for me; don't turn your back on me now. Don't throw me out, don't abandon me; you've always kept the door open. My father and mother walked out and left me, but GOD took me in.
PSALM 27:9–10 MSG

Some of us know the heartbreak that comes with a parent's rejection or abandonment. We know what it feels like to have someone we trust walk away. And while the pain in that moment feels unbearable, it's the gift that keeps giving well into our adulthood. Navigating the trauma becomes a barrier to trusting others.

Today, grab on to the beautiful truth that when someone you trusted left, God intervened. Right then and there, He scooped you up. He held you tight. And if you let Him, God will heal that wound in powerful ways. Push through the pain and courageously grab on to God. Anchor your faith in Him and watch as He puts the pieces of your heart back together.

Dear God, I'm trusting You to restore and heal my brokenness. Make me whole again so I can live unhindered by past pain. In Jesus' name I pray. Amen.

ON YOUR BEHALF

*And in a similar way, the Holy Spirit takes hold
of us in our human frailty to empower us in our
weakness. For example, at times we don't even
know how to pray, or know the best things to
ask for. But the Holy Spirit rises up within us
to super-intercede on our behalf, pleading to
God with emotional sighs too deep for words.*
ROMANS 8:26 TPT

Do you see the beautiful blessing unpacked in today's verse? God is not afraid of our weakness. It
doesn't frustrate Him or cause Him to turn away
from us, annoyed. Because He is our Creator, God
fully understands our human frailty and makes provision for it.

Don't stress about your prayers. They don't
need to sound melodic or follow a divine formula.
There are no right words or right ways to say them.
As a matter of fact, God understands our struggle
and His Spirit intercedes on our behalf. And when
words don't come, He already knows our hopes
and heartaches.

*Dear God, I am humbled and grateful that
You provide even in the times when I can't
articulate my feelings. Thank You. Amen.*

CALM, COOL, AND COLLECTED

Light, space, zest—that's GOD! So, with him on my side I'm fearless, afraid of no one and nothing. When vandal hordes ride down ready to eat me alive, those bullies and toughs fall flat on their faces. When besieged, I'm calm as a baby. When all hell breaks loose, I'm collected and cool.
PSALM 27:1–3 MSG

Imagine being calm, cool, and collected when chaos breaks out around you. Think about the confidence boost it would provide! Without your knees knocking and your hands shaking at every scary situation that comes your way, you'd stand strong with clear eyes and a brave heart.

What's the secret to this kind of living? It's recognizing that God is on your side. He is your shelter and strong tower. He is your rescuer and Savior. When you realize that God is always working for your good and His benefit, your heart can be at rest. You can experience peace that makes no sense to the world.

Dear God, I don't have to be afraid anymore. Even when things are crazy all around me, I can be calm, cool, and collected through faith. In Jesus' name I pray. Amen.

DETERMINED TO STAND

So, what does all this mean? If God has determined to stand with us, tell me, who then could ever stand against us? For God has proved his love by giving us his greatest treasure, the gift of his Son. And since God freely offered him up as the sacrifice for us all, he certainly won't withhold from us anything else he has to give.

ROMANS 8:31–32 TPT

There's no need to fear. Yes, that's often easier said than done. Life has a good right hook, doesn't it? But when you embrace courageous faith—understanding that God's presence is a mighty force—the difficult circumstances won't have power over you. Knowing that He's with you at all times will strengthen your confidence and help you weather the storm.

Where do you need to walk out this truth in your life right now? Is your name being dragged through the mud? Are you facing a lawsuit? Have you lost your job? Is an important relationship being challenged? Be brave, continually pray, and remember that God is determined to stand with you through it.

Dear God, thank You for standing with me— always. In Jesus' name I pray. Amen.

NEITHER LEAVE
NOR LET DOWN

"Be strong and courageous," David said to his son Solomon. "Get to work. Don't be afraid or discouraged, because the LORD God, my God, is with you. He'll neither let you down nor leave you before all the work for the service of the LORD's temple is done."
1 CHRONICLES 28:20 CEB

Do you know why you can do God's work with courageous faith? It's because He will not leave you to figure things out alone. God promises to be with you every step of the way, giving you the tools necessary to walk out the calling on your life. He won't let you down either. When you need God, He will be there. When you need guidance, He will provide it.

Knowing this frees you up to be strong and courageous. It will help keep you from giving in to discouragement, believing God is with you always. Let the knowledge of His presence make you bold in how you choose to live your life of faith.

Dear God, Your presence is a supernatural boost that keeps me full of confidence and courage. In Jesus' name I pray. Amen.

CONDEMNATION
OR CONVICTION

Who then is left to condemn us? . . . [Jesus] gave his life for us, and even more than that, he has conquered death and is now risen, exalted, and enthroned by God at his right hand. So how could he possibly condemn us since he is continually praying for our triumph?
ROMANS 8:34 TPT

Condemnation and conviction are not the same, and we need to know the difference between the two. Condemnation comes directly from the enemy. He uses it to shame us so we crawl back into the pit of despair, and we're left feeling weak, unlovable, and unworthy. Neither God nor His Spirit have anything to do with condemning feelings.

Conviction, on the other hand, is a gift from the Holy Spirit. He uses it to guide us away from old and negative behaviors. Conviction never leaves us feeling hopeless. Instead, it infuses us with strength and courage to make the right choices. It's how we learn righteous living.

Dear God, help me know the difference between condemnation and conviction so that my confidence grows in truth. In Jesus' name I pray. Amen.

RELAXED, CONFIDENT, AND BOLD

The wicked are edgy with guilt, ready to run off even when no one's after them; honest people are relaxed and confident, bold as lions.
PROVERBS 28:1 MSG

When people live and function honestly in community, life is so much more relaxed. Think about it. When you live authentically, you can be stress-free because you aren't trying to cover up any lies. You can be confident because you're not trying to be anyone but who God made you to be. You can be bold because you know you aren't trying to control or manipulate those around you.

Without God, chances are your life won't look like this. Instead, it might be marked with mean-spiritedness, bad choices, shame and guilt, and drama. You won't have access to the confidence and strength the Lord provides those who love Him. Let this contrast speak directly to your heart today, informing how you choose to live.

Dear God, help me live authentically, unafraid to be honest with others. Let me be as bold as a lion in my faith, living and loving well. In Jesus' name I pray. Amen.

142

THE ENDLESS LOVE OF GOD

Who could ever divorce us from the endless love of God's Anointed One? Absolutely no one! For nothing in the universe has the power to diminish his love toward us. Troubles, pressures, and problems are unable to come between us and heaven's love. What about persecutions, deprivations, dangers, and death threats? No, for they are all impotent to hinder omnipotent love.

ROMANS 8:35 TPT

How would you live differently if you knew nothing could separate you from God's love? Would you be more willing to step out of your comfort zone, knowing it could be messy? Would it free you up to be yourself? Would it get you off the performance treadmill of perfection?

Let today's verse sink deep into your heart, building your confidence. What a blessing to realize that God's love is unchangeable. It's unsinkable. It's irrevocable. It's unshakable. And no matter how badly we mess up, no matter the number of times we fail, His love stands.

Dear God, thank You for promising endless love toward me. My confidence is secure, knowing I can't mess our relationship up, for Your grace abounds! In Jesus' name I pray. Amen.

143

CLINGING TO GOD'S PEACE

I have told you these things so that you will be
whole and at peace. In this world, you will be
plagued with times of trouble, but you need not
fear; I have triumphed over this corrupt world order.
JOHN 16:33 VOICE

Many people think that being a follower of Jesus
means we will not face trials and tribulations. They
believe we will be saved from hardship. But that's
simply not true, and there is nowhere in the Bible
that confirms it. Instead, God's Word is clear that
we will have times of trouble. Life will be challenging. Our hearts will be broken. We will face
mountains and valleys. Thinking differently will set
us up for disappointment.

But we can take courage, knowing our faith
in God brings beautiful blessings. When faced
with difficulties, we can be confident because the
Lord has beat the world. He has overcome every
earthly obstacle for us. Anxieties, persecution, sin,
sorrow, and death have no power over us. Instead,
we can confidently cling to God's peace through
all our struggles.

Dear God, give me Your peace when the world tries
to overwhelm me. In Jesus' name I pray. Amen.

NO BEARING

So now I live with the confidence that there is nothing in the universe with the power to separate us from God's love. I'm convinced that his love will triumph over death, life's troubles, fallen angels, or dark rulers in the heavens. There is nothing in our present or future circumstances that can weaken his love.

ROMANS 8:38 TPT

The enemy loves to make us look down the road to see horrible outcomes and endings. He tempts us to see destruction ahead, filling our hearts with anxiety about the future. We stress about our financial health. We worry that fighting with our spouse will lead to divorce. We fear our kids will make terrible choices that will ruin their futures. And we worry that aches and pains will point to a devastating diagnosis.

Scripture says that neither your present nor future circumstances have any bearing on God's love. He can love you no more or no less than He does right now. You may not be confident in most things, but you can be fully assured of this powerful promise.

Dear God, what a relief to know nothing will change Your love for me. In Jesus' name I pray. Amen.

WHEN YOU DON'T FEEL BRAVE OR STRONG

Be brave. Be strong. Don't give up.
Expect God to get here soon.
PSALM 31:24 MSG

Sometimes it's hard to be brave. We get tired of having to put on our big-girl panties and push through once again. We have seasons when the barrage of badness feels overwhelming, causing us to lose our desire to keep going. We don't feel brave; we feel beat down. We don't feel courageous; we feel cranky. It's part of the human condition, and every single one of us struggles from time to time.

But all throughout God's Word we read the command to be strong and not give up. It is a consistent theme we can't ignore. If God says something once, pay close attention. But if He repeats it over and over again, hold it tight and recognize the weight of His words. And when you don't feel brave or strong, pray in expectation, asking for courageous faith.

Dear God, sometimes I feel weak. Give me confidence through faith so I can stand strong through anything. In Jesus' name I pray. Amen.

THROW YOURSELF ON GOD

Desperate, I throw myself on you: you are my God!
Hour by hour I place my days in your hand, safe
from the hands out to get me. Warm me, your
servant, with a smile; save me because you love me.
PSALM 31:14–16 MSG

Can you remember a time you faced a struggle so overwhelming you prayed every hour, maybe every minute, for God to intervene? Maybe someone you cared about was clinging to life in the hospital. Maybe you discovered your husband's betrayal. Maybe the moral failure was yours, and you were trying to figure out your next step. Maybe your child experienced unbelievable trauma. Regardless, God is there.

Let God be the reason your faith becomes courageous and bold. Let Him strengthen your bones so you can stand strong in the middle of your circumstances. Ask Him to renew you, rescue you, and restore you. In those desperate moments, throw yourself on God.

Dear God, help me remember to reach out
to You in desperate times. So often I go
silent because of fear. But instead, I will
throw myself on You, knowing You're mighty
to save. In Jesus' name I pray. Amen.

UNAFRAID OF BAD NEWS

They will not be afraid when the news is bad
because they have resolved to trust in the Eternal.
Their hearts are confident, and they are fearless,
for they expect to see their enemies defeated.
PSALM 112:7–8 VOICE

What does it look like to resolve to trust God? Does it mean you have a determination to trust that God is at work in your situation? Is there a steadfastness in your faith that proves unshakable when hard times come barreling at you? Do you choose to trust God over giving in to fear? Are you bold in your belief that the Lord is on the move and working things for your good and His glory?

It is possible to be unafraid when bad news comes, but it requires courageous faith that comes from God. Ask the Lord to strengthen your resolve to trust Him. Ask Him to make your heart confident and fearless. And ask Him to wrap His arms around you so you feel peace in the middle of the chaos.

Dear God, embolden my heart so I can stand
unmoved by the difficult circumstances I'm
facing. In Jesus' name I pray. Amen.

WHEN THE PAIN IS PERSONAL

*So don't be afraid. I am here, with you;
don't be dismayed, for I am your God. I will
strengthen you, help you. I am here with My
right hand to make right and to hold you up.*

ISAIAH 41:10 VOICE

As women, we navigate challenges every day personally and with our families. Most often we're capable of dealing with difficult circumstances ourselves, being solution oriented and remedy focused. But sometimes fear leads us into intimidation. We become dismayed and disheartened because we feel helpless.

At those times when the pain is so personal, our only hope is God. We get knocked to our knees, and only His strength gives us courage to find our footing again. Dig deep with God in those moments, praying with expectation that He will intervene. Let Him make right the wrong you are facing.

*Dear God, You know where my fear lies because
You know those secret places in my heart. You see
what intimidates me, causing distress. Make my
faith courageous and my belief in You bold so I can
trust You through it. In Jesus' name I pray. Amen.*

SHOWING GOD YOUR LOVE

Praise the Eternal! How blessed are those who revere the Eternal, who turn from evil and take great pleasure in His commandments.

PSALM 112:1 VOICE

One way to deepen your relationship with the Lord is through praise and worship. Scripture says that when we show reverence toward God, we will experience His blessings. Every decision we make to turn away from evil will be rewarded. Every time we choose joy in following His will and ways, we'll experience His delight.

How do you show God your love? How does He know how you feel about Him? What do your words and actions preach? Let this be a reminder to boldly declare His goodness in your life. Confidently share your story so others can see a road map to God. And commit yourself to praising His faithfulness, showing gratitude for keeping you on the right path.

Dear God, help me to be demonstrative in how I show You my love. Let me praise You every time I see Your goodness. Let me always respect and honor You with my life. I am so grateful that You're my heavenly Father! In Jesus' name I pray. Amen.

IN A MANNER WORTHY

Most important, live together in a manner worthy of Christ's gospel. . . . That way, you won't be afraid of anything your enemies do. Your faithfulness and courage are a sign of their coming destruction and your salvation, which is from God.

PHILIPPIANS 1:27–28 CEB

If your goal is to deepen your relationship with God, then make sure your life reflects that desire. This isn't always easy to do, because it takes boldness to align your words with your actions. It takes consistency every day, making hard choices at the crossroads life presents. And it requires faithfulness fueled through regular prayer and time in the Word.

Where do you need to make necessary changes in how you're living? What is the quality of community you're surrounded by? Are you finding courage to stand against hard seasons and difficult people? Before your feet hit the floor in the morning, ask God to help you live in a manner worthy of Christ's Gospel so that confidence radiates from the inside out.

Dear God, help me to be a loving and faithful woman who loves others well and glorifies Your name. In Jesus' name I pray. Amen.

BE LIKE A SNAKE AND A DOVE

"Stay alert. This is hazardous work I'm assigning you. You're going to be like sheep running through a wolf pack, so don't call attention to yourselves. Be as shrewd as a snake, inoffensive as a dove. Don't be naive. Some people will question your motives, others will smear your reputation—just because you believe in me."
MATTHEW 10:16–17 MSG

Through prayer, seek God's wisdom as you follow His will for your life. Be mindful of His leading so you stay on course, avoiding distractions or discouragement along the way. And remember that kind of courageous faith comes from God, so ask Him for it.

God will give you the grit to be as shrewd as a snake. He will give you the grace to be as harmless as a dove. And He will give you the confidence to be bold as you face any criticism for following His will. Remember that God will never call you to something without making every provision necessary for you to faithfully and courageously walk it out.

Dear God, give me courageous faith to do Your will. In Jesus' name I pray. Amen.

PRAISING GOD
THROUGH PRAYER

Yahweh, you alone are my inheritance. You are my
prize, my pleasure, and my portion. You hold my
destiny and its timing in your hands. Your pleasant
path leads me to pleasant places. I'm overwhelmed
by the privileges that come with following you!
PSALM 16:5–6 TPT

This scripture demonstrates what it looks like to
have a grateful heart toward the Lord. The psalmist
is being kind and generous through prayer, affirming
who God is in his life. Imagine how it must delight
Him to hear such thankfulness from His child!

Let the same be true in your life. Choose to
be persistent in praising Him every day. Let your
worship be what strengthens and deepens your
relationship. Be bold in your appreciation, recognizing the ways His hand has moved determinatively
in your life. And don't be shy in telling Him what
He means to you. Let your prayer life be rich with
times of sharing your love and adoration for your
heavenly Father.

Dear God, You are my prize, my pleasure,
and my portion. I'm so grateful to be loved
by You! In Jesus' name I pray. Amen.

THE GIFT OF HIS PERFECT PEACE

*"I leave the gift of peace with you—my peace.
Not the kind of fragile peace given by the world,
but my perfect peace. Don't yield to fear or be
troubled in your hearts—instead, be courageous!"*
JOHN 14:27 TPT

We all struggle to feel peace, especially in this day and age. By just watching five minutes of world news, we're stirred up and stressed out. Every day we encounter chaotic situations at home. We face tumultuous circumstances in the workplace. And those experiences leave us paralyzed with fear and terrified of the future.

Let prayer be your refuge. As you sit with God, unpacking your heart, His presence will wash over you. It will prove to be time well spent because you'll experience a peace that makes no sense to the world. They simply cannot replicate it. And with that peace will come a confident faith, making you ready to face the difficulties ahead. Instead of letting fear win, ask God for both courage and calm.

*Dear God, I confess I've looked to the world
for help and hope, but all I need is Your
perfect peace. In Jesus' name I pray. Amen.*

HEAD TO HEART

The way you counsel me makes me praise you
more, for your whispers in the night give me
wisdom, showing me what to do next. Because
I set you, Yahweh, always close to me, my
confidence will never be weakened, for I experience
your wraparound presence every moment.
PSALM 16:7–8 TPT

Today's scripture is another example of the value
we get from God's awesome presence. The Bible
is chock-full of reminders enticing us to connect
with His heart in meaningful ways. As women who
want to grow closer to our Creator, it's important
that we start by recognizing the blessings that come
from a deeper faith.

When we first become believers, God deposits
His Holy Spirit in us. That means His presence is
always there. But as we become more invested in
our relationship with God, we begin recognizing
His presence easier. It's not just head knowledge
anymore. It's heart knowledge. And that's where
our confidence comes from.

Dear God, let my faith in You become mature
enough that it penetrates the depths of
my heart. In Jesus' name I pray. Amen.

LET GO OF FEAR

When struck by fear, I let go, depending securely upon You alone. In God—whose word I praise—in God I place my trust. I shall not let fear come in, for what can measly men do to me?
PSALM 56:3–4 VOICE

Sometimes scripture feels lofty, like it's talking about things we feel ill equipped to handle. It challenges us to live in ways that feel foreign—ways opposite from how we've been living. But if we want a deeper connection with God and to grow our faith in Him, we'll follow His Word.

Fear is a big deal because it feels personal. It threatens parts of our lives that are important to us. But the psalmist gave fear to God rather than holding on to it. When fear struck, he passed it on to God. Notice the courage in his voice as he reminded himself of who God was to him. Let the same be said about you.

Dear God, give me courageous faith through my prayers for help. I give You my fear. In Jesus' name I pray. Amen.

THE ONE WHO DOES GLORIOUS THINGS

You will say on that day: "Thank the LORD; call on God's name; proclaim God's deeds among the peoples; declare that God's name is exalted. Sing to the LORD, who has done glorious things; proclaim this throughout all the earth."

ISAIAH 12:4–5 CEB

Tell the Lord "thank You." Let Him know you are grateful for His hand in your life. Let every prayer be full of gratitude, letting God know He is an invaluable part of your every moment. Just like any appreciative child, direct your words to glorify the kindness and generosity you've been shown because of His love.

Take time today to meditate on the compassion God has shown to you. Think back to difficult circumstances you've been in and look for evidence of His fingerprints. Ask for revelation of God moments as you revisit certain times in your life. And then boldly pour out your heart of thanks to the One who has done glorious things.

Dear God, let me always find the courage to give You the glory and proclaim Your deeds to the world. In Jesus' name I pray. Amen.

MY OFFERING

I am bound by Your promise, O God. My life is my offering of thanksgiving to You, for You have saved my soul from the darkness of death, steadied my feet from stumbling so I might continue to walk before God, embraced in the light of the living.

PSALM 56:12–13 VOICE

In the scripture above, what does "my life is my offering of thanksgiving to You" mean? It reads as if it's a response to God saving and steadying the writer so he could continue faithful living. Can you relate in your own life?

For those who love Him, God is the ultimate rescuer. He's the One who keeps us steady and focused as we traverse the rocky path of righteous living. He hears our persistent prayers for help and hope. And from a place of deep gratitude, it's our greatest desire to live in such a way that He is glorified throughout the heavens and the earth. That's our offering.

Dear God, my life is my offering of thanksgiving to You! You are my rock and my salvation, and my heart is full of thanksgiving. In Jesus' name I pray. Amen.

YOUR STRENGTH AND SHIELD

"God is indeed my salvation; I will trust and won't be afraid. Yah, the Lord, is my strength and my shield; he has become my salvation."

ISAIAH 12:2 CEB

What has you trapped in fear right now? Are you worried about a diagnosis that feels hopeless? Are you facing tremendous debt that seems insurmountable? Are you overwhelmed at work, worried that you won't be able to meet the deadlines set before you? Is your marriage in another challenging season that feels endless? Without a doubt, life's challenges test our foundation.

Don't forget that prayer is one of your greatest weapons against fear and discouragement. God is always listening and will come to your rescue when you cry out. Rather than trying to figure everything out on your own, let God be your strength and shield. Trust Him with your heart. Let Him fill you with courageous faith as you trust that He has your back.

Dear God, let my prayers reach Your throne room. Hear my shaky voice as I share the fear inside. I know that Your love will make me brave as I trust You to be my strength and shield. In Jesus' name I pray. Amen.

UNWAVERING FAITH THAT GOD CAN

"If our God—the one we serve—is able to rescue us from the furnace of flaming fire and from your power, Your Majesty, then let him rescue us. But if he doesn't, know this for certain, Your Majesty: we will never serve your gods or worship the gold statue you've set up."
DANIEL 3:17–18 CEB

This is courageous faith defined! Shadrach, Meshach, and Abednego faced a tyrannical king who demanded they go against God and obey him instead. Nebuchadnezzar threatened to throw them into the fiery furnace for disobeying him, but these three men stood their ground and put their full trust in God. They knew God could save them, but if He chose not to, their faith wouldn't waver.

Time invested with the Lord brings about this kind of courageousness. Time in His Word, in prayer, and in praise yields this kind of unwavering faith in God's ability. It will also create in you the belief that God is still good even if He doesn't respond in the way you expect Him to.

Dear God, make me bold and brave.
In Jesus' name I pray. Amen.

WHEN YOU FEEL OUTNUMBERED

"Be brave and be strong! Don't let the king of Assyria and all those warriors he brings with him scare you or cause you dismay, because our forces are greater than his. All he has is human strength, but we have the LORD our God, who will help us fight our battles!"
2 CHRONICLES 32:7–8 CEB

Sometimes what scares us the most in difficult situations is that we feel outnumbered. We feel like the lone voice of reason, and that intimidates us. Sometimes it shuts down our willingness to speak out. Sometimes we respond by hiding out. Sometimes we feel weak and just give up. This is when we need to talk to God the most.

Through prayer, God will give you courageous faith to be brave and strong even when you don't see a way out. We need this because our humanity brings frustrating limitations we can't overcome. Without His presence, we simply don't have what it takes to stand victorious.

Dear God, give me strength to be strong and brave, knowing You are with me always. In Jesus' name I pray. Amen.

HOW DO YOU HANDLE A CRISIS?

If you fall apart during a crisis, then you
weren't very strong to begin with.
PROVERBS 24:10 VOICE

How do you handle a crisis? Do you shine, able to navigate the mountains and valleys with confidence? Do you crumble? Do crises make you feel weak and unable to make sense of anything? Consider that your response to hard circumstances is a direct result of the depth of your relationship with God. Your ability to navigate difficult moments well depends on the maturity of your faith.

Ask God daily to infuse you with courageous faith. Ask Him to transfer strength to your character. Ask for resolve. Tell Him of your need for endurance, especially perseverance for long-suffering. And commit to deepening your relationship with the Father through prayer and time in the Word, because that's where all the power for a life of courage comes from.

Dear God, thank You. I realize now how
important it is to be anchored securely
to You. In Jesus' name I pray. Amen.

THE CHOICE IS YOURS

"Come and join me," Jesus replied. So Peter stepped out onto the water and began to walk toward Jesus. But when he realized how high the waves were, he became frightened and started to sink. "Save me, Lord!" he cried out. Jesus immediately stretched out his hand and lifted him up and said, "What little faith you have! Why would you let doubt win?"
MATTHEW 14:29–31 TPT

Peter was a pillar of faith and an important part of Jesus' public ministry, spending time on the front lines with Him. He knew Jesus was the real deal. And he believed with all his heart that Jesus was the Messiah his people had been waiting for. Yet even Peter chose to take his eyes off the Lord, giving in to fear.

If you're not trusting God every day, your courageous faith will be temporary. Trusting God when you're scared is a choice you make. So ask the Lord to strengthen your resolve to choose wisely!

Dear God, grow my trust in such a way that when faced with a choice, I always side with faith. In Jesus' name I pray. Amen.

THE GIFT OF MEMORY

*Revel in his holy Name, GOD-seekers, be
jubilant! Study GOD and his strength, seek
his presence day and night; remember all
the wonders he performed, the miracles and
judgments that came out of his mouth.*
1 CHRONICLES 16:10–12 MSG

Your memory is a powerful tool for encouraging
your faith. When we find ourselves in the middle of
a heartbreak or trauma, we need something to hold
on to. We need a reminder of God's sovereignty
and goodness. And looking back at the wonders
He has performed in your life does that. Recalling
miracle moments emboldens your faith that He
will do it again.

Today, ask God to bring those times to mind.
Did He restore a relationship? Did He meet a need
in unexpected ways? Did He open or close a door?
Sit in the details, unpacking the arduous circumstances where He intervened. And thank Him for
leaving a record you can revisit when you need a
boost of faith.

*Dear God, I love being able to remember
examples of Your kindness and generosity
in my life. Thank You for the gift of
memory. In Jesus' name I pray. Amen.*

PASS IT ON

Joshua told them, "Don't hold back. Don't be timid. Be strong! Be confident! This is what GOD will do to all your enemies when you fight them."
JOSHUA 10:25 MSG

Joshua told the Israelites to be strong in battle. He told them not to hold back, for God was with them and for them. Why do you think Joshua was so bold in his command? Most likely it was because God's directive to be bold and courageous had finally gotten through to him and he saw the need to pass his courageous faith along to the people.

We can share our courage and faith with others as well. As we deepen our relationship with God, our faith grows stronger. In your prayer time, ask God to show you people who need encouragement to be brave and reminders to be confident. And then cheer them on as they take the next steps forward in obedience to the Lord.

Dear God, thank You for encouraging me to be strong and confident in my faith. Use me to pass it on to others by opening my eyes to see who needs reassurance. In Jesus' name I pray. Amen.

BEING A CATALYST FOR COURAGE

Be strong, and let us fight bravely for the sake of our people and the cities of our True God, and may the Eternal do what seems good in His sight.
2 Samuel 10:12 voice

Sometimes we have no choice but to be courageous in the face of difficult circumstances. God often uses the faithful to defend the weak and downtrodden. Just as Joab, the commander of David's army, was spurring on the men for the battle, we may be the ones God uses to motivate others for what's ahead.

Do you feel ill equipped to be as bold as Joab? Ask God to embolden you for the job He's asking you to complete. Trust Him to give you the right words to be a catalyst for courage. And remember that if the Lord is trusting you to inspire and invigorate bravery in others, you can confidently step up to the challenge, for He will equip you. That's a promise.

Dear God, help me to believe that You will bless me with the divine toolbox as I obediently walk out the call You've placed on my life. In Jesus' name I pray. Amen.

WORKING TOWARD THE HARVEST

Don't allow yourselves to be weary in planting good seeds, for the season of reaping the wonderful harvest you've planted is coming! Take advantage of every opportunity to be a blessing to others, especially to our brothers and sisters in the family of faith!
GALATIANS 6:9–10 TPT

When you want to give up, dig in deep through prayer and ask God for perseverance. Every time you want to throw in the towel, be persistent in your request for His help. Because when you choose to stick it out, boldly believing that God will strengthen your resolve, a wonderful harvest will be waiting on the other side.

This means you work through marital problems even when your marriage seems a lost cause. It means you continue parenting your difficult child, staying vigilant and engaged. It means you speak out against injustice, waiting for the truth to come out. And it means you continue praying for answers until you get one.

Dear God, give me perseverance to stay the course faithfully so I can reap the wonderful harvest. In Jesus' name I pray. Amen.

WHEN FAMILY NEEDS SAVING

*Because I know all these things, this is my request:
Since I have treated you kindly and have protected
you, please promise me by the Eternal that you
will do the same for my family. Give me some
sign of good faith that when you destroy this city
you will spare my father and mother, my brothers
and sisters, and their families from death.*
JOSHUA 2:12–13 VOICE

Imagine the courage of Rahab. Not only did she
protect the foreign spies as they entered her city,
but she also boldly asked for a favor in return. And
like any woman would do, she thought of her family and asked for them all to be spared during the
attack on the city.

You can be bold as you're praying for family.
And when you're asking for them to be saved from
something, God hears you. It may be an addiction
or a mental illness or a difficulty at school. There's
nothing too big or too small. But pray confidently,
knowing that God has a plan.

*Dear God, give me courage to ask for Your help for
those closest to me. In Jesus' name I pray. Amen.*

FOR GOD'S APPROVAL ONLY

Let everyone be devoted to fulfill the work God has given them to do with excellence, and their joy will be in doing what's right and being themselves, and not in being affirmed by others. Every believer is ultimately responsible for his or her own conscience.
GALATIANS 6:4–5 TPT

Working for the approval of others is dangerous. Wanting to be recognized for a job well done is a common thread that knits us together as women, right? But we're being challenged by today's scripture to make sure our hearts are in the right place as we do God's work. Our desire for excellence should be an offering to God rather than an opportunity to impress others.

Ask God to give you a heart set on devotion to Him. Let the Lord build in you a confident faith by knowing that He delights in your obedience. And ask God for a divine reminder to check your motives as you walk out the call He has placed on your life.

Dear God, let me work to honor You rather than to be affirmed by others. In Jesus' name I pray. Amen.

STEADFAST CONFIDENCE

So now, beloved ones, stand firm, stable, and enduring. Live your lives with an unshakable confidence. We know that we prosper and excel in every season by serving the Lord, because we are assured that our union with the Lord makes our labor productive with fruit that endures.

1 CORINTHIANS 15:58 TPT

When our focus is on serving the Lord with the work we do, we will prosper. God rewards those who are obedient, who follow His desire for their lives. Even when we mess up, God sees hearts motivated to please Him and blesses them. And we can rest assured our desire to serve is a direct result of time spent in His presence.

Even more, loving the Lord creates an unshakable confidence to withstand the mountains and valleys of life. God is the One who gives us the ability to do His will and follow His ways. So don't forgo time in prayer or time in His Word, because your persistence will pay off.

Dear God, all I want is for the work of my life to point others to You. In Jesus' name I pray. Amen.

THE HARVEST

*The harvest you reap reveals the seed that you
planted. If you plant the corrupt seeds of self-life
into this natural realm, you can expect a harvest
of corruption. If you plant the good seeds of
Spirit-life you will reap beautiful fruits that
grow from the everlasting life of the Spirit.*

GALATIANS 6:8 TPT

What kind of seeds are you planting in your life?
Are you kind to others? Are you generous with time
and treasure? Do you purpose to make others feel
loved? Is compassion part of your life as you care
for the needs of others? Is your faith courageous?
Are you bold in your belief, helping others stand
strong too?

Scripture says that what we sow, we reap. If
we're planting seeds that glorify the Lord, our harvest will be reflective of that. So be very careful
about what you allow into your life. Let God be
the gardener plucking any weeds that threaten
the crop of goodness.

*Dear God, help me to be confident about what
seeds I'm planting, knowing they will directly affect
the harvest of my life. In Jesus' name I pray. Amen.*

ARE YOU KEEPING GOOD COMPANY?

So stop fooling yourselves! Evil companions will corrupt good morals and character. Come back to your right senses and awaken to what is right. Repent from your sinful ways. For some have no knowledge of God's wonderful love. You should be ashamed that you make me write this way to you!
1 CORINTHIANS 15:33–34 TPT

Have the courage to keep good company, because you are who you hang out with. It's not always easy to end relationships that are toxic or unhealthy, but faith should drive us to surround ourselves with those who point us toward God. Not because we are better than others, but because we want to pursue righteous living.

Do you need to make some changes in your community? Ask God to make you bold as you turn from sinful ways and from those who lead you in the wrong direction. Ask for courage to stand your moral ground, doing what you know pleases God.

Dear God, help me surround myself with people who love You. And give me wisdom and discernment as I navigate relationships. In Jesus' name I pray. Amen.

BOLD FAITH TO SPEAK UP

*Queen Esther answered, "If I please the king,
and if the king wishes, give me my life—that's
my wish—and the lives of my people too. That's
my desire. We have been sold—I and my people—
to be wiped out, killed, and destroyed. If we
simply had been sold as male and female slaves,
I would have said nothing. But no enemy can
compensate the king for this kind of damage."*

ESTHER 7:3–4 CEB

Esther risked her life by speaking so boldly to her
husband, the king. But she had courageous faith,
believing it was her destiny to speak up on behalf
of her people who were targeted for extinction.
She was emboldened to do what was right.

The more time you spend with God, the stronger your faith will grow. And mature faith will allow
you to stand up against evil. It can be uncomfortable to follow God's plan, but that's why we ask
for courageous faith. Ask Him for what you need
each step of the way, and watch how you make a
difference for the kingdom.

*Dear God, make me brave to speak
up. In Jesus' name I pray. Amen.*

IS MONEY YOUR GOD?

Your way of life should be free from the love of money, and you should be content with what you have. After all, he has said, I will never leave you or abandon you. This is why we can confidently say, The Lord is my helper, and I won't be afraid. What can people do to me?
HEBREWS 13:5–6 CEB

Investing our hope in anything the world offers is a lost cause. Of course, we need money to make ends meet, but when it becomes our god, let it be a red flag. Our goal should not be to collect more toys but to invest in the kingdom in meaningful ways.

Our contentment doesn't come from cars or homes or vacations or the like. If we truly understood the gift of God's presence, our hearts would be full every day. Every investment you make in your relationship with God through prayer or time in the Word draws you closer to Him. Let that be enough. Let it be what satisfies.

Dear God, help me want You the most— more than anything the world promises will fulfill! In Jesus' name I pray. Amen.

YOUR SOUL IS SECURE

"Listen, my beloved friends, don't fear those who may want to take your life but can do nothing more. It's true that they may kill your body, but they have no power over your soul."
LUKE 12:4 TPT

What a relief to know no one or nothing can snatch your soul from God. You are secure in His hands, and He will not let go. Let that truth encourage your heart today, especially quieting the voices that stir up fear inside. While your body may be at risk, your relationship with God never is. You can rest easy with that truth today.

Spend time today thanking God for His unending love. Thank Him for promises that anchor you to His heart. Ask the Lord to fill you with the kind of faith that's bold in its belief of His faithfulness. And every time you begin to worry, let God be the One to bring comfort, reminding you that you're safe.

Dear God, because I have decided to follow You, I am able to rest in the truth that nothing can separate me from Your love. In Jesus' name I pray. Amen.

MAYBE EVEN AN ANGEL

*Let love continue among you. Don't forget to
extend your hospitality to all—even to strangers—
for as you know, some have unknowingly shown
kindness to heavenly messengers in this way.*
HEBREWS 13:1–2 VOICE

Want a good reason to be courageous in your faith?
Consider that you may cross paths with an angel—a
heavenly messenger sent from God. So when you
have an opportunity to step outside your comfort
zone and bless someone, don't hesitate. Keep an
eye out for bold ways to show compassion. And
lead with confident generosity, always willing to
give of yourself.

The deeper the relationship with your Father,
the more natural it will be for you to love others
with ferocity. It will be an organic overflow of time
invested with God. Don't forgo connecting to His
heart in meaningful ways, because it's from that
place that you will bless those around you—maybe
even an angel.

*Dear God, let my life be an extension of
Your goodness to everyone I meet. Open
my eyes to see the needs before me, and
give me the courage to put myself out there
to help. In Jesus' name I pray. Amen.*

ACKNOWLEDGING JESUS PUBLICLY

"I can assure you of this: If you freely declare in public that I am the Son of Man, the Messiah, then I will freely declare to all the angels of God that you are mine. But if you publicly pretend that you don't know me, I will deny you before the angels of God."
LUKE 12:8–9 TPT

Never shy away from acknowledging God publicly, because doing so will have natural consequences you won't want to face. Instead, be ready and excited to share your testimony of God's goodness and faithfulness every chance you get.

Speaking up may be hard. You may be nervous to let others have a peek inside your life. So ask God to give you a fearlessness when it comes to sharing the Good News. Many times our ability to be bold and authentic comes directly from God Himself. So don't hesitate to ask Him to fill you with courage so you can boldly profess the truth of Jesus rather than give in to timidity.

Dear God, Your Son is worthy of my public recognition! In His name I pray. Amen.

MORE GRATEFUL THAN SURPRISED

"My God sent his messenger, who shut the lions' mouths. They haven't touched me because I was judged innocent before my God. I haven't done anything wrong to you either, Your Majesty." The king was thrilled. He commanded that Daniel be brought up out of the pit, and Daniel was lifted out. Not a scratch was found on him, because he trusted in his God.

DANIEL 6:22–23 CEB

Daniel recognized that God was the reason he wasn't devoured in the lions' den. Everyone knew the big cats were there specifically to kill those sentenced to death. The lions understood the drill, and they'd be ready to do the job when the opportunity presented itself.

So consider that Daniel was more grateful than surprised he survived the night. He was a faithful servant in a hostile land, maturing his faith through persistent prayer and making it courageous. He trusted God to save his life if that was His plan. Be like Daniel—a bold believer steeped in prayer and a heavenly perspective.

Dear God, fill me with courage and confidence in who You are and the promises You've made. In Jesus' name I pray. Amen.

WHEN COMMUNITY IS HIS PROVISION

Esther sent back her answer to Mordecai:
"Go and get all the Jews living in Susa together.
Fast for me. Don't eat or drink for three days,
either day or night. I and my maids will fast
with you. If you will do this, I'll go to the king,
even though it's forbidden. If I die, I die."
ESTHER 4:15–16 MSG

Esther knew she needed reinforcements. Going before the king meant risking her life, so she asked for the help of her countrymen. Sometimes there is safety in numbers, requiring an entire community of believers to rise up together to spur courageous faith. Esther knew this was necessary for the task ahead.

Don't be afraid to ask for help when you need it. God gave us family and friends for a reason. And there are times when people are His provision for life's difficulties. As you pray, ask God for discernment to know when to rally the troops and when your faith should be in Him alone.

Dear God, thank You for blessing me with
community. Help me to know when and how to
utilize them in my life. In Jesus' name I pray. Amen.

CONSUMING THOUGHTS

"Perfect, absolute peace surrounds those whose imaginations are consumed with you; they confidently trust in you. Yes, trust in the Lord Yahweh forever and ever! For Yah, the Lord God, is your Rock of Ages!"

ISAIAH 26:3–4 TPT

In a world where we have responsibilities and deadlines to maintain and meet, how are we able to let our imaginations be *consumed* with God as the verse above mentions? Maybe it's not an either/or. Maybe what it's suggesting is that we invite God to be part of the details in our lives. Maybe it's weaving a continuous conversation throughout the day, talking to God about what's on our hearts and minds.

When we keep the Lord at the front of our thoughts, we become fully aware of His presence. And throughout the Word, we learn that because God is with us, we're able to have confidence and courage. And peace. Start your morning with a prayer, and let it continue until your head hits the pillow at night.

Dear God, grow my faith stronger and bolder as I talk to You all day long. In Jesus' name I pray. Amen.

WHO GOD IS TO YOU

Blessed be the Eternal, my rock. He trains my hands for war, gives me the skills I need for battle. He is my unfailing love and my citadel. He is my tower of strength and my deliverer.
PSALM 144:1–2 VOICE

Think of how confident you would be knowing today's scripture as indisputable truth. How would it change your perspective if you truly believed what the psalmist was saying? To know that God will give you every skill needed for battle should increase your courage tenfold. To understand that He will give you life experiences that will train your hands for war should make you bold. And then to realize that no matter what, you are loved, you are protected, and God will deliver you from evil helps your heart to be at peace.

Spend time in prayer asking God to make these beautiful realities come alive in your life. Meditate on them. And let these truths strengthen your relationship with the Father, because He is with you and for you always.

Dear God, let these truths bring hope to my heart and courage to my faith. In Jesus' name I pray. Amen.

THE PATH

The path of the righteous is smooth and level;
God, the Just One, you make a clear path
for them. Yes, we will follow your ways, Lord
Yahweh, and entwine our hearts with yours, for
the fame of your name is all that we desire.
ISAIAH 26:7–8 TPT

Chances are you've found yourself on a crooked, muddy, uphill path several times throughout your life. It's been laced by difficult relationships, financial troubles, health challenges, parenting woes, and debilitating fear and insecurity. As you look back on those times, where was God?

When we commit our lives to following Jesus, He doesn't guarantee a problem-free existence. Instead, the promise is that He will be with us through those hard times. He will give us tools to navigate the twists and turns when we go to Him in prayer. He will equip us to trust Him in the valleys and on the mountaintops. And we'll receive courageous faith to follow His lead as He smooths the path before us.

Dear God, let me be quick to come to You in
prayer as I wait for Your guidance on the path
I am walking. In Jesus' name I pray. Amen.

GUT-WRENCHINGLY HONEST

*Send forth bolts of lightning, and scatter my
enemies. Shoot Your fiery arrows, and rout
the enemy. Reach down from Your high place;
save me out of the great waters; rescue me
from the grasp of these foreigners who speak
only lies and don't have truth in their deeds.*
PSALM 144:6–8 VOICE

Have the courage to ask for God to show up in a
big way. Dream big, letting Him know the kind of
display you're hoping to see play out in your life.
Cry out to God through persistent prayer and let
Him know your desperation. Tell God you need to
be saved. Ask to be rescued. Share your desire for
the Lord to bring justice to those who have hurt you.

It is safe for you to be gut-wrenchingly honest
with God. Nothing you ask will make Him think any
differently of you. And the deeper your relationship
with the Lord, the freer you will feel to be boldly
authentic in your prayers.

*Dear God, thank You for the freedom to pray
with passion about how I'm feeling and what
I'm needing. In Jesus' name I pray. Amen.*

PLEASING GOD WITH YOUR CHOICES

You can avoid evil through surrendered worship and the fear of God, for the power of his faithful love removes sin's guilt and grip over you. When the Lord is pleased with the decisions you've made, he activates grace to turn enemies into friends.

PROVERBS 16:6–7 TPT

Scripture says it is through our reverence for God and our humble worship that we can sidestep evil. Think about what it would take for worship to be integrated into your day. If you are intentional to honor God with your choices and quick to praise His hand moving in your circumstances, you will have little time to get yourself into trouble. Amen?

Living a life that is pleasing to the Lord fosters confidence. It becomes the lens you look at life through, making decisions that will keep you pursuing righteous living. So let your prayer life reflect this desire and ask God to keep you focused on making bold choices that reflect your faith.

Dear God, help me live with passion and purpose so my life blesses and glorifies Your name. Give me courage to make the right choices. In Jesus' name I pray. Amen.

GOD'S LOVE NEVER QUITS

Thank God because he's good, because his love never quits. Tell the world, Israel, "His love never quits." And you, clan of Aaron, tell the world, "His love never quits." And you who fear God, join in, "His love never quits."

PSALM 118:1–4 MSG

Believing that God's love for you will never end takes courageous faith. Why? Because we have all experienced the end of someone's love before. Maybe a parent walked out on you. Maybe a husband filed for divorce. Maybe a best friend left you behind. Or maybe your love for someone began to wane and you're the one who gave up.

Even though you've felt the pain of rejection before, in His Word God promises to love you forever. Through prayer, ask Him to solidify this truth in your heart. Ask for tangible reminders when you need them most. And let God bring this promise to life so any past rejection doesn't keep you from boldly believing that His love for you is everlasting and unbreakable.

Dear God, help me to overcome past heartaches so I can embrace the beauty and power of Your love. In Jesus' name I pray. Amen.

GOD IS FOR YOU

*Out of my deep anguish and pain I prayed, and
God, you helped me as a father. You came to my
rescue and broke open the way into a beautiful and
broad place. Now I know, Lord, that you are for
me, and I will never fear what man can do to me.*
PSALM 118:5–6 TPT

Sometimes it takes a miraculous act of God for us
to recognize with certainty that God is for us. Be
it because of our stubbornness or our unbelief, we
often need reminders to secure a confident faith
that His love is unchanging. God's Word says that
nothing can separate us from Him. And it offers
countless assurances that His plans for our future
are good.

Let God solidify this truth in your heart through
time spent in the Bible and in persistent prayer.
Get to know Him as your Father. And then bravely
cry out in those difficult and painful moments with
expectation, certain He will rescue you. Let the
Lord prove He is *for* you!

*Dear God, give me the spiritual eyes to
see all the ways You show Your love and
approval. In Jesus' name I pray. Amen.*

WITH THE RIGHT MOTIVES

*You are jealous for something you can't get,
so you struggle and fight. You don't have
because you don't ask. You ask and don't
have because you ask with evil intentions,
to waste it on your own cravings.*

JAMES 4:2–3 CEB

We are encouraged to persist in prayer, asking God for the things we need to help us navigate the ups and downs of life. He is always listening and ready to respond in the right ways at the right time. So often what we think we need and what God knows we need are two different things. And so part of having courageous faith means we trust His answers and timing.

Today's scripture reminds us to double-check our intentions when asking God for help. If our motives are selfish, indulgent, or disingenuous, God will keep us out of harm's way by refusing to give us what we ask. In love He will answer based on His wisdom. Be blessed knowing we can trust the Lord's response to our prayers.

*Dear God, I trust You to answer my prayers
with holy discernment, knowing what's best
for me. In Jesus' name I pray. Amen.*

187

PRAYING WITH AUTHENTICITY

"When you pray, there is no need to repeat empty phrases, praying like the Gentiles do, for they expect God to hear them because of their many words. There is no need to imitate them, since your Father already knows what you need before you ask him."

MATTHEW 6:7–8 TPT

This passage is a fantastic reminder that our prayers don't have to follow any formula to be heard by God. We don't have to find the right words to unpack what's on our hearts. And even if we don't know how to describe our feelings, we can trust that God already knows every detail.

Choose to be authentic with the Lord, not putting on airs as you pray to Him. Find the courage just to be honest, even if it's messy. And let your conversations be what deepens your relationship, building a confident faith that you are loved and valued by the One who created you.

Dear God, I'm grateful You're a safe place for me to share the things on my heart— things I can't tell anyone else. Give me confidence and courage to be authentic as I talk to You. In Jesus' name I pray. Amen.

SCRIPTURE INDEX

MORE INSPIRATION FOR
YOUR BEAUTIFUL SOUL

God Calls You Worthy
978-1-64352-474-0

God Calls You Loved
978-1-64352-804-5

God Calls You Forgiven
978-1-64352-637-9

God Calls You Chosen
978-1-64352-926-4

God Calls You Beautiful
978-1-64352-710-9

These delightful devotionals—created just for
you—will encourage and inspire your soul with
deeply rooted truths from God's Word

Flexible Casebound / $12.99 each